Reminiscences of
Rudolf Steiner
and Marie Steiner-von Sivers

Ilona Schubert

Temple Lodge Press, London

First English edition 1991

Originally published in German under the title *Selbsterlebtes im Zusammensein mit Rudolf Steiner und Marie Steiner* by Zbinden Verlag in 1985.

© Dr C. Polzer, Dornach, Switzerland.
This translation © 1991 Temple Lodge Press.

All rights reserved. No part of this publication may be reproduced in any manner whatsoever without the prior permission of Temple Lodge Press, 51 Queen Caroline Street, London W6 9QL.

Translated by John M. Wood
Cover design by S. Gulbekian

Cover picture: Rudolf Steiner 1918
© Verlag am Goetheanum, Dornach, Switzerland

A catalogue record for this book is available from the British Library

ISBN 0 904693 31 7

Typeset by DP Photosetting, Aylesbury
Printed and bound by
The Cromwell Press Limited,
Broughton Gifford, Melksham, Wiltshire

Contents

	Introductory Note	1
1	My First Encounter with Rudolf and Marie Steiner and with Eurythmy	2
2	The Start of My Eurythmy Career in Dornach	10
3	The Beginnings of Tone Eurythmy	17
4	Group Work and Solo Pieces	20
5	New Impulses, New Tasks	25
6	About Make-up	28
7	Eurythmy in the Goetheanum Building	29
8	Eurythmy Tours	35
9	Actors and Helpers in Dornach	40
10	The Burning of the First Goetheanum	45
11	Reverence Towards the Goetheanum	49
12	Dr Steiner's Illness and Death	50
13	The Work of Frau Dr Steiner After Dr Steiner's Death	54
14	Experiences at the Theatre	57
15	Remarks by Dr Steiner About Various Pictures	66
16	Episodes	76

17	Eurythmy Lessons with Children from 3 to 7 Years	79
18	Remarks by Dr Steiner About the Twelve Virtues	84
19	Meditation for the Sick and Dying	85
20	Remarks by Dr Steiner Concerning Pregnancy and the Care of Young Children	86

Introductory Note

The reporting of what I experienced in the company of Rudolf Steiner and Marie Steiner can only be accomplished out of a feeling of the deepest gratitude for my destiny which allowed this meeting to take place.

After having been asked many times to write down my experiences, which I have often spoken about, I do so here with great pleasure. The personal human details may appear to be trivial, but I hope that what I have written will add some enlivening touches to the picture we have of Rudolf Steiner.

Ilona Schubert
28.3.1900–26.10.1983

1. My First Encounter with Rudolf and Marie Steiner and with Eurythmy

After having read the basic works of Rudolf Steiner and attended an introductory course given by Herr Adolf Arenson, I was allowed to travel to Stuttgart to hear Dr Steiner himself speak. That was in April 1918. I had received my membership card from Rudolf Steiner at Christmas 1917. Our group leader in Mannheim, Frau Helene Röchling, wife of the privy councillor, and my mother both said that I was much too young and that no one could become a member before the age of 21. Now it so happened that I was in lodgings in Weimar in 1917 and had lessons there in History of Art, History and Literature from the assistant director of the Goethe House. When the latter noticed my enthusiasm for everything connected with Goethe, he allowed me to come into the Goethe House whenever I wanted. He explained many things to me there, especially in the natural-scientific section which was of particular interest to me at that time—for instance, Goethe's colour theory and his discovery of the intermaxillary bone. And I was allowed—sometimes even unaccompanied—to enter Goethe's workroom or the little garden at the back of the house. So I was often in the library where Dr Steiner had also worked. Full of enthusiasm, as only the young can be, I wrote home about all my experiences. My mother showed these letters to Dr Steiner, whereupon he allowed me to become a member of the Society at such an early age.

During that first lecture in Stuttgart I sat in the front row to one side of the stage and Dr Steiner glanced my way several times. After the lecture he came up to me and asked: 'Could you follow?' I replied shyly and a little confused by the fact that he addressed such a young person as me: 'Yes, Herr Doktor, a little.' 'Well, that will get better as time goes on,' he said, 'and now I will take you to Frau Dr Steiner.' Frau Dr Steiner was still seated, conversing with others in the front row, and when I stood in front of her after having been introduced she looked at me for quite a long time and then asked: 'What are your particular gifts?' Very much taken aback by such an unexpected question I could only blurt out, 'Gifts, Frau Doktor? I don't really have any.' With a smile she said to me, 'But I hear that you have had

Rudolf Steiner
27.2.1861–30.3.1925

Marie Steiner-von Sivers
14.3.1867–27.12.1948

Erna Bögel
6.9.1877–16.9.1963

Helene Röchling
28.1.1866–14.8.1945

a musical training and are very fond of dancing.' I confirmed that. It was evident that she had been told that by my mother. Frau Doktor then went on to say: 'Wouldn't you like to come to our little eurythmy performance tomorrow? Perhaps you will find it so nice that you would like to join us.' So that is how I came to see a eurythmy performance for the first time.

It was a small stage. To one side of it were several lady eurythmists sitting on a bench dressed in simple white garments with a kind of penitent's cord around their waists—that was the sort of impression I had to begin with. At a given signal they stood up and walked slowly and solemnly onto the stage with the gesture of devotion (arms crossed in front of the breast). Then Frau Doktor started to recite and the eurythmists moved in accordance with it. That made an overpowering impression upon me who had only been used to seeing 'dancing' to music. It stirred me in a very special way, with such force that I could have cried or laughed. Well, I was still very young and so I laughed, which drew upon me the censuring looks of those around and later the reprimands of my mother. 'That is the last time I am taking you to a eurythmy performance!' she said. But there was nothing laughable about it in my mind. The laughter was only the reaction to very strong feelings.

I can still feel today how moved I was. As soon as I reached the hotel I said to my friend, who had also been present at the demonstration, 'Come, we'll have a little practice!' I put the chairs and table aside and we attempted to imitate what we had seen. When my mother came into the room later she asked: 'Whatever have you been up to?' I told her: 'We are trying to do eurythmy and I *have* to learn it properly right away.' When Frau Dr Steiner heard about it next day she said: 'I didn't expect anything else!' And three days later, when I was back in Mannheim, I got a teacher, Fraülein Edith Röhrle. During the next fortnight we practised eurythmy just about every day from early morning until evening. I learnt to step, to follow rhythms, to do the sounds and to run Apollonian and Dionysian forms. That was rather difficult on the waxed parquet dance floor of our house—it would be unthinkable today, but at that time the pace was much slower. In practising the prelude 'Behold thyself—behold the world', I experienced the very heart of eurythmy. I felt completely changed, as though I had grown out beyond myself. The *inside* and the *outside* became concrete experience. Even today I can recall the bliss of that moment.

Soon afterwards I returned to Stuttgart to Dr Steiner's lectures. At that time I was allowed to take part in the eurythmy practices which took place in a little pub near the Landhausstrasse. In those days Frau Dr Steiner did the exercises with us. There were a lot of rhythms, threefold walking and rod exercises, and we did eurythmy to spoken poems. The lady teachers took it in turn to recite. As this was the time in which Emil Molt made his decision to found a school for the workers of his Waldorf Astoria cigarette factory and begged for suggestions and advice from Dr Steiner, he was told that he should introduce eurythmy into the general school curriculum. In order to show the workers' families what eurythmy was all about, a demonstration was arranged on a grand scale. So we gathered together daily in the Landhausstrasse to prepare for it. I was also allowed to take part in the basic exercises. The demonstration took place on 22 June 1919 in the Arts House, the so-called 'Goldenen Hirsch' [Golden Hart] in Stuttgart. Two days previously one of the eurythmists had sprained her ankle and now something happened to me which has often occurred since in my life: I had to take her place at short notice. Among other things I had quickly to learn a part in a humoresque, namely that of Bim in Christian Morgenstern's 'Bim-Bam-Bum'. Dr Steiner drew a little form (unfortunately no longer in existence, but copied by me) and showed me several different movements. I then practised most of the day with 'Bam' and 'Bum' and Dr and Frau Dr Steiner thought that it would be all right.

For this performance, which was literally our first appearance on the stage, Dr Steiner himself made us up, and he dealt very lavishly with the make-up equipment. We felt very strange with all that paint on us. The performance went well and was received with a great deal of applause. At the final item—namely, 'Bim-Bam-Bum'—I had the misfortune to be the last one on the stage and was unable to find the exit through the heavy velvet curtain. I ran along the curtain feeling about desperately but could not find the opening! That must have looked very comical, for the audience clapped louder and louder as I became more and more confused. At last one of the eurythmists behind the stage noticed that something was wrong and that I had not returned. She hurried to my rescue and drew me forth from my prison. Later Dr Steiner came backstage and said, 'You did that excellently, it was a splendid exit.' I, on the other hand, wept

Ilona Bögel as 'Bim'
in 'Bim, Bam, Bum' by Christian Morgenstern

and said, 'I'm never going on the stage again.' Frau Dr Steiner said laughingly, 'Perhaps you still might consider it.' Well, I have often been on the stage since, over many years, but the fear of not being able to find the exit has never completely left me. Immediately after the performance Emil Molt treated us to a big party where we all received lots of flowers and cigarettes.

When I returned once more to my home town I at once received further lessons; this time my teacher was Fräulein Erna Wolfram (the later Frau van Deventer). During this period too we worked the whole day through. At the same time I read all Dr Steiner's basic works, attended lectures and took introductory courses in Anthroposophy. I also continued with my music studies, but this only by the way. So October 1919 drew on and I was to go to Dornach for the first time. I was overjoyed at this, yet on the eve of departure I cried my eyes out without being able to say why. It dawned on me later that it was a leave-taking of my homeland and the start of a new stage in my life. We actually only intended to spend a fortnight in Dornach, but I was immediately involved in very intensive eurythmy work, so that Frau Dr Steiner asked me if a return to Mannheim was really necessary or if I would not prefer to devote myself entirely to eurythmy. And so I stayed in Dornach, where I remained until this day.

2. The Start of My Eurythmy Career in Dornach

We arrived in Dornach one late October afternoon. After taking our things to our lodgings we immediately made our way up to the Goetheanum. A rehearsal for the first scene in Faust's study was in progress in the Workshop. All eyes turned towards us as we entered the darkened room. Dr Steiner interrupted the rehearsal, came towards us and said, 'So here is Ilona with us at last. That is a blessing.' He led me to Frau Dr Steiner and allowed me to sit beside her on a little dais. The rehearsal proceeded. Herr Stuten was on the stage taking the part of Faust. As he reached for the cup with the poison Dr Steiner interrupted him, quickly made his way onto the stage to which a small wooden staircase led from the auditorium—how often I witnessed the lightness of his step in later times when he sprang onto the stage to show how a passage should be performed—and acted the whole scene over again. Unforgettable for me was the part where Faust reaches out towards the cabinet and with the words 'And now come down thou cup of crystal clearest', takes off the cover and, slightly in profile as if he were already standing at the threshold between this world and the next, slowly raises it on high, gazing into the distance lost in thought, before putting it to his lips. Then he said to Herr Stuten: 'To create the right mood this pause and the gesture should be prolonged as much as possible.' The rehearsal ended with this advice.

Next morning I travelled to town and as I was looking in the shops a lady approached me and asked if I could sing. When I said yes she replied, 'Good, then come to the rehearsal this afternoon and you can take part in the *Faust* choruses.' This lady was Fräulein Käthe Mitscher, who was indispensable for the stage work at that time. She was responsible for everything; she saw that the musical scores were laid out on the desks, and that everyone appeared for the rehearsals and performances at the right time and was provided with the written texts for the various items. She also recited at the rehearsals and part-rehearsals when Frau Dr Steiner herself was not present. There was in fact nothing over which she did not keep a watchful eye. Busy from morning till evening she nevertheless managed to attend to all the personal requirements of the eurythmists, actors and musicians. Although she possessed the true humour of the people from Cologne she could nevertheless be very strict. In the years to follow she was often in charge of the eurythmy tours. She would then make arrangements in the various theatres—often under very difficult circumstances—and would even take responsibility for the lighting. She saw to the accommodation of the artists and ensured that everyone was fairly treated and under her exemplary command everything always turned out perfectly. The tours during the first years (1920–24) were mainly to Germany and were often very difficult to arrange on account of the inflation, delayed trains, and other things connected with the aftermath of the war. After the opening of the First Goetheanum, Fräulein Mitscher took over the office of stage-manager and continued with it until her death in 1940.

I now return to Fräulein Mitscher's invitation to me to join the choir practice. I did take part in the singing on that occasion but, as we were singing behind the scenes, I was not able to see the performance and it made me sad. When Dr Steiner heard about it he said, 'No, that is not right, you must see the performance from the auditorium for once. Later there will be plenty of opportunity to join in.'

So I sat in the front row on Sunday afternoon and followed what happened on the stage with great delight. It impressed me so deeply that I remained sitting and sobbing in my place after the curtain had fallen. Dr Steiner came up to me, laid his hand on my shoulder and said, 'It is good that you are so deeply moved. It *is* a magnificent scene isn't it?'

I must add, however, that the whole thing was arranged in the most primitive fashion, with a relatively small stage, black curtains, a small desk, a small cabinet, a skeleton and a very small dais in the background. After Faust had raised the cup to his lips the Easter bells started to ring. For a moment all was dark. When the stage lit up again the black curtains had been changed for red ones and all was shining with a bright light. The Angels were arrayed on a raised platform, Frau Kisseleff with a crowd of older and younger children who performed eurythmy to the spoken choruses. Also the women and disciples were portrayed in eurythmy. Each chorus was preceded by the singing of the Angels. It all worked so powerfully in its simplicity.

My eurythmy career started in Dornach the next day. Here, too, as in Mannheim, I was given eurythmy lessons by a lady teacher—there were no eurythmy schools at that time, and in this instance it was Fräulein Groh who taught me. I had an hour's lesson every day in the early morning. Then we usually had a rehearsal from 10.00 till 11.00 under the guidance of Frau Kisseleff, with whom it was so nice and harmonious to work. On these occasions we were wont to practise the new pieces which would then be elaborated with Frau Dr Steiner who came every day at eleven o'clock. Frau Doktor nearly always brought new forms with her for solos or group work and then the places were allotted to us. It was always exciting to discover who was allowed to take which part. Nearly all of us were involved in the bigger pieces, as we were only a small group of eurythmists.

To begin with Frau Doktor reviewed what we had been practising

Tatiana Kisseleff
15.3.1881–19.7.1970

Käthe Mitscher
9.5.1882–9.4.1940

Jan Stuten
15.8.1890–25.2.1948

and then she corrected us. It always amazed me how she was able to give the right touch to a thing with only a few words. But she never let anything go until we had succeeded in carrying it through to her satisfaction. Now and again it was the cause of tears. Once when I had tried something over and over again and Frau Doktor was still not satisfied with me, nearly blinded with tears I was on the point of resigning when she said to me: 'Yes, art is difficult and the best we can achieve is won at the cost of tears and despair. It is not art to look charming when one is young and is able to move freely, but to hit on the right style and to be able to sink oneself into the personality of the particular poet or musician, *that* is true art.' She recommended, for instance—yes, even demanded from us—that we should study the biographies of the poets and musicians. Dr Steiner once said to me: 'It would contribute much to the success of a performance if, before it starts, one were to visualize how the poet or composer looked and in what age he lived and what his surroundings were like.' I always practised that and found it very helpful. Dr Steiner then usually turned up at about half past twelve or one o'clock to take Frau Doktor to lunch, but on such occasions he was shown what we had practised and then he often gave us special instructions. If a eurythmist had to study a new piece of music she would then ask Dr Steiner for a form. Then he asked for the piece to be played and during this time he drew the form. In cases where the piece of music had several voices or was played on several instruments he asked for it to be played over and over again until he had drawn forms for each part. We watched him from in front, from behind and from the side and in our enthusiasm drew nearer and nearer to him until in desperation he called out, 'But leave me at least a space for my drawing.'

The rehearsals continued in the early afternoon. They usually commenced with solo pieces and then continued with group work. At five o'clock Frau Doktor came while we were all practising and towards seven o'clock Dr Steiner joined us and the proceedings continued almost without end. It was only on Fridays and Saturdays that we finished earlier, for those were the days which had been set aside for Dr Steiner's lectures. We gave smaller or larger performances fairly regularly on Saturdays and Sundays in the afternoons. On those occasions the pieces we had already performed were repeated and a few new items were added. Thus we had an opportunity of repeating things many times and Dr Steiner told us that we must perform a thing at least fifty times until we were really sure of it.

On lecture days we eurythmists and musicians and whoever else was involved in the rehearsals had their supper served in what was known as the Golden Man, a connecting passage between the dressing-room and the auditorium running alongside the stage. This name was given it in fun by Dr Steiner at the conclusion of a humoresque by Christian Morgenstern called 'The Unicorn' in which the line occurs: 'Then we sit in the Golden Man and say our solo piece.'

3. The Beginnings of Tone Eurythmy

During the first years it was mainly speech eurythmy that was done. With this were the so-called 'preludes' which prepared the way for the various moods of the text and were accompanied by music. Tone eurythmy was still in its infancy. A piano teacher, Fräulein Hollenbach, also taught songs at this time which the children sang in a most charming way, and little minuets by Bach and Mozart which they performed with tone eurythmy and presented from time to time at the end of the main programmes. What one chiefly had at that time were the indications by Rudolf Steiner for movements in connection with the scales and tones for major and minor. Tones were then practised either standing or hopping, and regrouping took place during the intervals. In contrast to the more advanced speech eurythmy, this can be described as primitive.

I often took part in these exercises, but in the long run this way of doing things did not satisfy me. One day I went to Dr Steiner and asked him if it would not be possible to make proper forms for tone eurythmy. He thought for a while and then said, 'Of course it would be possible. Have you any ideas about how to do the hopped tones?' Now I had already been trying out various things on my own and I demonstrated these to him, whereupon he was quite satisfied. Then he asked me if I already had a piece of music in mind and, as I had been practising Grieg's *The Butterfly* on the piano, I immediately said, 'Oh yes, *The Butterfly* by Grieg.' 'Good,' said Dr Steiner, 'let me hear

Ilona Bögel
in *The Butterfly* by Ed. Grieg

it played tomorrow.' As, however, I had to go away the next day it was Fräulein Hollenbach who played it to him and a few days later I received a letter from her containing two forms drawn by Dr Steiner and a note saying that I should try out both of them and choose the one I liked best.

On my return to Dornach I practised very hard and soon I was able to show Herr and Frau Dr Steiner what I could do. There then followed questions, such as, for example, how the quick runs should be performed. Now in this instance, as in so many later ones, Dr Steiner did not say or show a person from the outset how things should be done. He expected people to develop their own ideas on the subject. In this particular case, in which a rapid succession of notes occurred, I struck the first note precisely and expressed the others by raising or lowering my arms. When I demonstrated this to Dr Steiner he said, 'Yes, that is very good, that gives a feeling for the pitch.' In the case of the more compact motifs, I chose to use what are called the 'small' tones, and that was also accepted by Dr Steiner.

Once Dr Steiner came into the room as I was practising on the stage in the Workshop. He stopped for a moment and watched what I was doing. Then at a certain moment he gave a shudder and pulled a face. I stopped to reflect, looking at him questioningly and he said, 'Why do you always do an F sharp there, it should be an A.' And of course he was right! How often have I thought since when we were doing tones—if all the wrong notes gave Dr Steiner such pain, what agony he must sometimes have suffered!

I should just like to add the following to this story about *The Butterfly*. When I first performed this number on the stage—it was the concluding piece in the programme, performed in the Goetheanum—Dr Steiner came backstage, gave me his hand and said, 'I wish to thank you most warmly.' I answered, quite taken aback, 'But Herr Doktor, it is I who have to thank you!' 'No,' he said, 'it is always something to be grateful for when new ideas come from the artists themselves, and what you have here brought signifies a further step in tone eurythmy.' I also performed *The Butterfly* several times in Stuttgart. The first time I did it there was tremendous applause. After I had taken several curtain calls Dr Steiner, who was sitting in the audience, came up to the footlights and said, 'Please do it again.' So I performed it a second time. Since that time it has been customary to give encores whenever there is a lot of applause.

4. Group Work and Solo Pieces

In connection with *The Butterfly* (it really has a story attached to it), I can quote another example of Dr Steiner's strict code of discipline. Before the start of a performance in the 'Wilhelma' in Bad Cannstatt the pianist told me that he had forgotten to bring his Grieg music with him. Someone immediately volunteered to go and fetch it, as there was plenty of time. But Herr Doktor, who heard about it said, 'No, that will never do. Before a performance *everything* must be to hand. It does not do to forget anything. We will just have to do without *The Butterfly* today.' The pianist said, 'But I can play *The Butterfly* by heart.' But even that was forbidden by Dr Steiner. 'Don't you understand how it is? If we wish to show the world something worthwhile then everything, really everything, has to be thought about *beforehand*.' Thus he often gave us hints for disciplining ourselves which stuck in our minds for the rest of our lives.

Something else which Dr Steiner regarded as a lack of discipline was the clicking of fingers to draw attention to oneself. Once when he heard this he gave a noticeable start and said crossly, 'You must never do that again. It is a very bad habit and causes annoyance. And when teachers click their fingers in class it is not only an ugly sound but it also has a bad effect. One should pay special attention to what one does with one's fingers.' It makes a good deal of difference in eurythmy whether one uses the thumb, forefinger or middle finger, or whether one makes use of the ring finger and little finger. When, as sometimes happens, there are no special indications as to which fingers to use, the fingers should be kept close together. To do eurythmy with the fingers spread out is extremely ugly and gives the impression of a kind of vanity. But in a humoresque, when such an effect is intended, it could be appropriate. Dr Steiner even suggested once that if it had become a habit which was hard to break, then one ought to put an elastic band round the fingers during rehearsals until one had learned to overcome it. In many characterizations where one wished to represent spiritual beings or elementary beings, he gave special indications in which only the index finger and middle finger should be used or the thumb, index finger and middle finger.

Perhaps I might also repeat a saying of Dr Steiner's to the effect that before every meditation the hands should be washed and that during the same or while listening to mantric texts one should never have one's arms or legs crossed. It is a typical feature of our time that when people sit down they automatically cross their legs and usually fold their arms. From the aspect of eurythmy that is an 'E' gesture [pronounced 'eh' in English] which expresses self-defence or even a shutting in of oneself.

Another case of a lesson on the subject of thoughtlessness was given to us by Dr Steiner before the start of a eurythmy performance in the Workshop. One of the lady eurythmists was adjusting her dress and veil in front of a mirror before going onto the stage. She tried out a few movements and spoke some of the words to herself. This was noticed by Dr Steiner who just then happened to be passing by on his way to the auditorium. Then a thunderstorm broke over the head of the poor eurythmist. We all rushed together in consternation. Seldom had Rudolf Steiner been so aroused. He kept on repeating, 'How can you possibly do such a thing? One must never do eurythmy in front of a mirror, you will ruin everything, your eurythmy will be killed if you do that, don't you understand? How can you be so thoughtless! All of you ought to feel that.' Even to the suggestion that she had only wished to see if the dress and the veil hung right when she moved, Dr Steiner said, 'Even that is not right, you still made several eurythmy gestures to sounds, and that is something quite impossible. If you want to see if everything is in order, you have enough fellow eurythmists who can give you their appraisal and advice.' The eurythmist was quite shattered, but all of us took that very much to heart. After the performance, which turned out very well in spite of the shock, Dr Steiner came behind the stage and was then extremely kind. He called us all together once more and said: 'You will understand that I had to make such a scene. It has to do with a quite definite and important piece of knowledge. You should think about this very carefully.'*

Nearly all the big group items were produced during 1919 and

---

* I am quite aware of the fact that, in describing this episode, I am, as it were, 'talking out of class'. But as I have undertaken to recount my experiences in my work with Dr and Frau Dr Steiner, I mention this episode too, which belongs very much to the theme. Such mistakes as this can happen to anyone in the most varied situations in life and one cannot emphasize strongly enough how strictly Rudolf Steiner adhered to the maintaining of responsibility, discipline and the careful attention to his advice.

1920. First came the forms, based mainly on 'regroupings in space'. They were constructed to such poems by Goethe as his 'cloud poems', *Hymnus an die Natur* [Hymn to Nature], *Metamorphose der Pflanzen* [The Metamorphosis of Plants], *Meine Göttin* [My Goddess], *An den Mond* [To the Moon], and *Mai-lied* [May Song]. A further series of 'regroupings' resulted in forms for *Chören der Urträume* [Choruses of Primal Dreams] and *Chören der Urtriebe* [Choruses of Primal Urges] by Fercher von Steinwand. Out of these there developed the so-called 'standard' forms. From then on we received a new form every time for the 'Weekly Verses', which up till then had been performed by Apollonian forms. In addition the eurythmists were given forms for their solo pieces which included instructions for special effects, chiefly head positions but also certain hand or finger movements and occasionally we were asked to do complicated jumps while running forms.

I was given very many complicated head positions for my solo pieces and Dr Steiner often moved my head into the right position and showed me how I should hold or move my hands if I did not at first understand what he intended me to do. In one of my solo pieces, a movement from a Beethoven sonata, I had to direct my gaze alternately onto my thumb and onto my big toe. The following happened to me during this procedure. At a certain point the melody divides into two parts and I was struggling to do all the notes simultaneously using both arms. It was a weary task and I practised for hours on end and was quite proud of my achievement. When I demonstrated it to Dr Steiner he said: 'Whatever are you doing? That is not right. You would not be able to sing two parts at the same time, would you? And, after all, tone eurythmy is "visible song". If you want to do something in two or more parts then get other eurythmists to do it with you.' In order to avoid misunderstanding I should like to add here that it is actually possible to present two parts in eurythmy by using the one or the other arm alternately, as for instance in the case of an upper and a lower voice, but then it must be carried out *one after the other* and not simultaneously.

The first solos I had to do were *Die Freuden—(Libelle)* [Pleasures—(The Dragonfly)] and *Cicade* by Goethe, *Das Vöglein* [The Little Bird] by Hebbel and *An mein Kalb* [To my Calf] by Fercher von Steinwand. When we did collective pieces I often had to take the parts of ants, beetles, butterflies and suchlike creatures—a thing which I enjoyed doing—but one day I did actually ask if I would *always* have to take the parts of animals as I would *so* much like to do something different for a change. Frau Dr Steiner said, with an amused smile, 'Yes, yes, Ilona would like to be a "Cassandra".' Well, I was not aiming as high as that, but Dr Steiner said, 'Yes, she will get *her* "Cassandra".' And what should that be? On the next day I was allotted *Die Spröde* [The Prude] and *Die Bekehrte* [The Convert] by Goethe. And it was in practising these poems that the event happened which I have already described when Frau Doktor was never satisfied with me and I was on the point of giving up. Afterwards they became my favourite pieces. In the following years I was given many solo pieces of this kind including, for instance, *Mit einem gemalten Band* [With a Painted Ribbon] and *Tage der Wonne* [Days of Bliss], both by Goethe, and also other poems.

It happened after a public lecture in the Sieglehaus in Stuttgart, when the applause had died down, that Dr Steiner called out in the hall, 'Is Fräulein Bögel here?' When I made answer he said to me, 'Please come with me to the car, I have something to say to you.' Then I had to go with him to the Landhausstrasse, where at suppertime Dr Steiner drew a form for me for the poem by Albert Steffen *Lasst uns die Bäume lieben* [Let Us Love the Trees]. Then he said, 'Now, go onto the stage and practise that.' Frau Dr Steiner came a little later and recited it for me and after some further time Dr Steiner came and gave me a few more instructions. After I had practised for some time he said, 'This poem is needed for tomorrow's programme and if you practise hard tomorrow morning it should be all right.' So I had from late one evening until the next afternoon to learn a new poem. But in the end it turned out quite well. This sort of thing is of course exceptional. As a general rule a piece has to be studied for a very long time, as is illustrated by the following story of *Das Vöglein* [The Little Bird].

When I was given the poem *Das Vöglein* by Hebbel, Dr Steiner showed me many head positions. For every verse—and they are very short—I had to do six different positions. At first I found that very difficult. There was no difficulty in just running the forms, or in doing the head positions on their own, but to do both things at the same time and to form the sounds as well just did not seem possible. Already after the third verse I became so giddy that I just staggered about. When, after long practice, I began to despair I said to Dr

Steiner, 'What shall I do?' He calmly replied, 'Go on practising.' I tried anew every day and in the end I was ready to give up. Rather cross about myself I decided to give it one more try. To *know* the form and sounds and head position was not enough, so I tried not to think any more about my head. Then behold! Suddenly I had got it. I succeeded in doing the whole poem in one go.

Overjoyed, I rushed to the Studio where Dr Steiner was working and knocked on the door. Too late I noticed what I had done. I had interrupted Herr Doktor at his work! I would willingly have withdrawn in the hope that he might not have heard me, but already the door had opened and Dr Steiner stood before me. I apologized profusely, but he was most friendly and said, 'I have been waiting for this to happen for a long time. You have succeeded, haven't you? I will come along presently and you can show me what you have done.' He closed the Studio door and accompanied me to the practice room.

When I demonstrated the poem to him he was most satisfied with it and said: 'Now, tell me how it came about that you can now do it.' 'Yes, Herr Doktor,' I said, 'it is very strange, I simply saw the little bird in front of me, first of all down on the right, then down on the left, and so on, just as you showed me with the head positions. With the last movement of my head I gave a little nod of pleasure.' (This last was recorded in the instructions as: 'Nod!') Then Dr Steiner said, 'Well, you see, I am very glad that you hit upon it yourself. I could have told you at the beginning, but I wanted you to find it out for yourself. And in future you should always do it in that way. You must *visualize* all you do in eurythmy as a picture in front of you. Only then does it become living eurythmy.' To his question about the appearance of the little bird, I said: 'Strangely enough it was a yellow bird.' 'So,' said Dr Steiner, 'that is very nice,' and he allowed me to wear a delicate little yellow veil for the performance. He praised me and thought it a good idea of mine to keep the gestures very small and to let them usually accompany the head movements.

This episode really helped me, and my many years of experience have taught me just *how* important it was that Dr Steiner let me 'flounder about' for so long on that occasion. That happened during my first Dornach period. I was together with a lot of older people about whom I knew that they had all been given personal meditations by Dr Steiner. As I also was 'keen to learn' I went straight up to Dr

Steiner in all my youthful unashamedness as he was standing in front of the Goetheanum and asked him if I could not also be given a meditation of my own. He looked at me in a friendly way and then said, 'But you have eurythmy.' When I looked at him rather enquiringly he then asked, 'Well, you *do* have it, don't you?' 'Yes, of course, Herr Doktor,' I said. 'Well then, you already have what you are asking for, don't you?' Only much later it dawned on me that Dr Steiner meant that eurythmy is not just a beautiful art but, if it is understood aright, it is also a path of training, namely, a way to attain to Imaginative vision. In order, however, to progress further in one's development it is obvious that one needs to do other meditations too.

5. New Impulses, New Tasks

There were new impulses and new tasks for us nearly every day. There was tremendous creativity and activity. The greatest seriousness gave way to the most delightful humour. There was often much to laugh at. During those rehearsals given us by Frau Dr Steiner alone, we were able to observe how exactly she had understood every detail of the often very brief instructions drafted by Dr Steiner and then had worked them out with us in such a magnificent way. And how pleased she was if Dr Steiner approved of what she had done. She also developed many new ideas of her own and then asked Dr Steiner for his opinion about them. He often took up an idea from Frau Dr Steiner and carried it further.

In 1921 Marie Steiner rehearsed the 'Merlin' from the *Woodland Poems* of Nikolaus Lenau. Dr Steiner had given her the eurythmy forms for it. Tatania Kisseleff took the part of Merlin. I was the Queen of the Elves. And also there were two Elemental Beings in this performance taken by Assia Turgenieff and Natascha Pozzo.

At the end of one of the rehearsals we were joined by Dr Steiner, for whom the whole poem was re-enacted. When our demonstration had come to an end Marie Steiner asked him what kind of music would be suitable for it, to which Rudolf Steiner replied: 'Well now, what about *The Flying Dutchman* or *Tristan?*' Marie Steiner called out in astonishment, 'What? Lenau and Wagner?' 'No,' said Rudolf Steiner, not Lenau and Wagner but Merlin—Wagner!'

After a while Marie Steiner repeated the words 'Merlin—Wagner' and then again, as if she had just realized something, 'Ach, Merlin—Wagner!' And then she asked, 'Is Richard Wagner Merlin?' 'Yes,' said he, 'it is so. You can get an inkling of it from his music.'

For a long time we were all very quiet. Greatly impressed, we thought deeply about what we had heard.

I do not remember any more what music was played for the 'Merlin' poem. It was certainly not anything by Richard Wagner for, as Rudolf Steiner emphasized when he was asked about it, this does not lend itself for use with eurythmy.

In practising Goethe's poem *Weltseele* [World-soul], Frau Dr Steiner wanted to take it at a rather quick pace. The forms were arranged in three concentric circles so that the eurythmists in the outer circle had to run particularly quickly. We rushed with rather large steps and arrived breathless. Dr Steiner observed us for a while and then said, 'Do not make such giant strides. That looks very ugly and you don't achieve anything. Take a lot of small steps and you will see that you are able to run quicker and with less effort, and apart from that the whole movement will gain in alacrity and lightness.' And also in the case of a cheerful poem he once said: 'Why do you always take such long strides? Don't let you feet be so lazy. It makes it look very clumsy. With every movement you must remain flexible.'

In the first years of eurythmy all forms were run concentrically, that is to say, the participants faced the centre of the room. As the work progressed, the possibility arose of directing the movements towards the periphery. In such a case it was the head which led the way and the body followed after. We first learnt to practise it in this way with the 'Romantic Prelude'. Dr Steiner first gave the form and then Herr Schuurman wrote a piece of music to it. In running the form in this way one felt as if one were being gently lifted out of the body. One's soul was then interwoven with a feeling of romance. To begin with we slightly exaggerated things so that Dr Steiner had to say to us: 'But do not sweep the floor with your heads.'

Just how far we had to be conscious of which type of movement we had to apply in which case, the following example will show. It gave us great pleasure at that time to use this new kind of movement-in-space wherever possible. One of the groups had been practising one of the 'Weekly Verses' in this way. The group had worked very hard at it and was looking forward to showing Dr Steiner what it had done. The result was shattering! The eurythmists in question were not even allowed to complete their piece when Dr Steiner called out: 'What you are doing is something terrible. You are losing yourselves completely in your surroundings and do not *experience* anything at all. That is not the way to present the "Weekly Verses" or anything else with a purely spiritual content. If one wants to do such texts in a way directed to the periphery one must never lose one's connection with the centre!' And he forbade not only this group but *all* groups to do any work connected with the 'Weekly Verses' for half a year, and he emphasized moreover that he had been forced to be so strict with us in order to impress upon our consciousness the feeling of responsibility which we must bear towards the spirit of eurythmy.*

In representing luciferic and ahrimanic beings this second form of movement was the appropriate one. One had to fall out of the centre, so to speak, and feel oneself drawn to the one or other side. We had practised doing movements for these beings for a long time and thought we had achieved something by our efforts. But Dr Steiner merely made a single laconic remark to us: 'Your Lucifers are like noodles and your Ahrimans like pocketknives. They should be lightning flashes and serpents.' We were quite in despair, but Frau Dr Steiner came to our rescue once again by suggesting that we should try to put ourselves in the place of these beings, in order to transcend the human and not remain too 'physical'. Yes, that was one of the most difficult things to do! Likewise the representation of elemental spirits is a very difficult task to perform. An example of this may prove very instructive. When we were practising the part of the Elves in *A Midsummer Night's Dream* in which we had to make rotary movements with our heads as well as to run the forms, we very soon began to feel dizzy. When we asked Dr Steiner what we should do about it, he said: 'Yes, that means that you are doing it in just the right way. You *should* actually lose yourself a little and deviate from what is human.'

---

* See previous footnote (p. 21).

6. About Make-up

It seems appropriate at this point to say a few words about make-up, because I have so often been asked about it. We first have to distinguish between the normal technique of making up and what can be called 'character portrayal'. For eurythmy performances Dr Steiner used to cover the whole of the face with an even layer of red on top of a natural skin-coloured base. At first the colours were rather vivid; later on they were modified to suit the lighting or the individual complexion. In the beginning the lighting was done by Ehrenfried Pfeiffer, but in later years by Georg Wurmehl and his helpers. The eyebrows followed the lines of the person's own eyebrows. In earlier times they were drawn in brown or even black, but later always in blue. In my case Dr Steiner drew a thin red line beneath the blue eyebrows. In the corners of the eye a little red spot was added and the bottom edges of the nostrils were tinted red. In the case of those with high foreheads the brow would be reddened slightly at the base of the hair and for those with low foreheads it would be made lighter with white greasepaint or powder. The neck should not appear too white in contrast to the rest of the face and should be shaded. The mouth followed the natural lines. In general the face as a whole should not undergo much change. But when, for instance, a person has very deepset eyes, that should be harmonized with a little make-up. The final procedure of course was the application of a thin layer of powder.

It was rather different in the case of character portrayal. For Fercher von Steinwand's poem *An mein Kalb* [To my Calf]—known as *Kälbchen*—Dr Steiner made up my forehead with a thick layer of white and drew red circles about my eyes along with a thickly plastered round red mouth and no other colours. With this there went a brown woollen dress without a girdle which had a white oval painted on the upper part. For our role in a humoresque called *Elstern* [Magpies], Dr Steiner painted the whole of our faces with crowsfeet like large Vs, which he then extended over the neck as well. For this he used a black pencil on which he pressed heavily. As it was very warm that day and we had to do a lot of hopping, you can imagine what we looked like at the end of the performance. During those first years there was occasionally a lack of water in the Workshop during the summer and, after we had removed our make-up with grease, a wash in warm water would have been most welcome. As it was, we had to wait for that until we got home and there was much amusement on account of our appearance! For the Black King of the Christmas play it was of course not much better. How I and others were made up by Dr Steiner for the part of Mary in the Christmas play I shall tell you later.

For the Angels in *Faust* we were given high rounded eyebrows on top of rosy countenances. The luciferic beings were heavily made up in red with very high eyebrows, that is, rising steeply from the nose and then sloping downwards to the sides. The lips were painted a vivid red. For ahrimanic beings a face shaded in grey had black lines down the cheeks and the corners of the mouth sloped downwards, the whole to give a hard, angular effect.

The Sirens in *Faust* had pale foreheads with red rings around the eyes and white rings around those, and a white line extending halfway down the nose. The mouth was not made up at all so that in that way the bird nature was emphasized. For a Japanese poem, I tried to make myself up to look like a Japanese woman. In things of that kind each one had to find out for herself how she should be made up. Herr Stuten became the expert in the art of make-up and was often asked for his advice.

7. Eurythmy in the Goetheanum Building

During the course of the years 1919 and 1920, the scaffolding in the First Goetheanum began to be removed. When I arrived in Dornach people were not allowed to enter the main hall unless they had work to do there. But Dr Steiner once took me with him onto the scaffolding and explained to me the architraves, capitals and the painting in the small cupola. It was a wonderful experience to be up there with Dr Steiner in the place where he had always worked. When the scaffolding was removed the next job was the seating. The eurythmists were then allowed to help with the painting of the seat numbers. We were not allowed to take part in the carving because

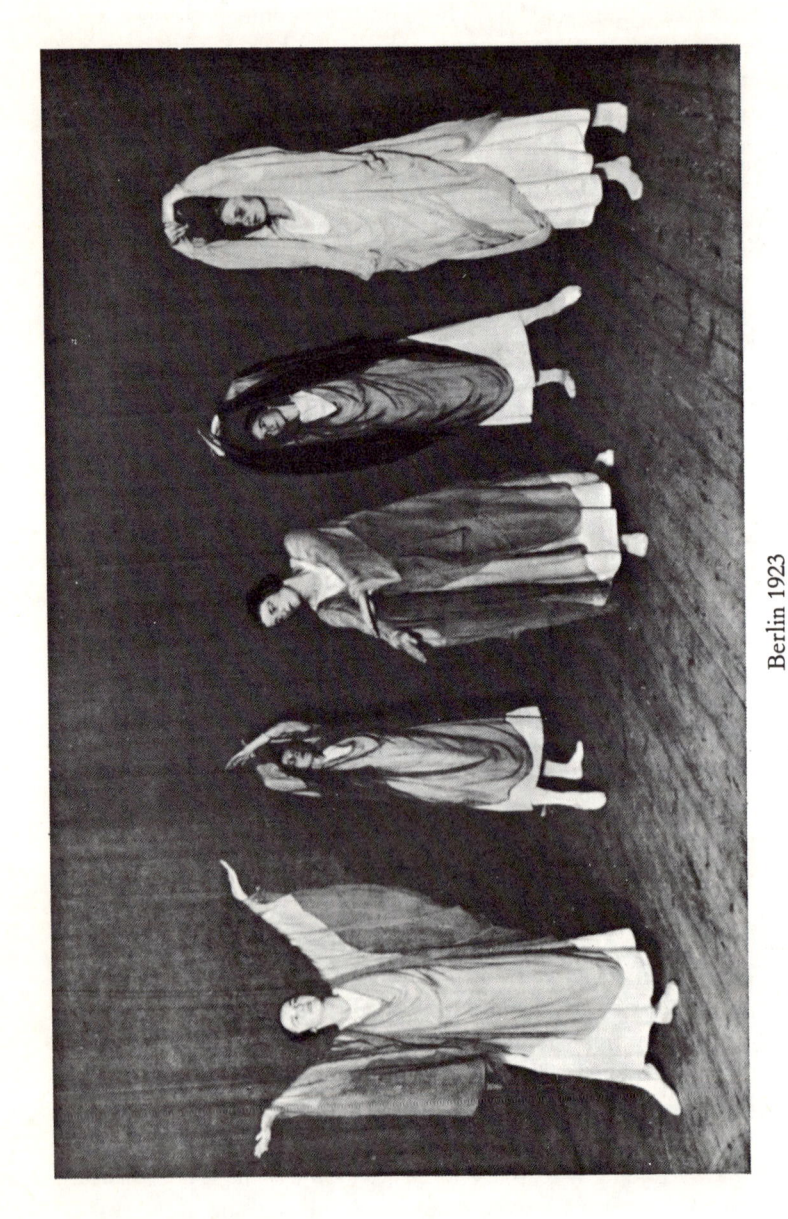

Berlin 1923
from left to right: Ilse von Baravalle, Natalie Pozzo,
Maria Ina Schuurman, Friedel Simons, Isabella de Jaager

Oxford 1922
upper row, from left to right: Tatiana Kisseleff, Mita Waller, Isabella de Jaager, Marie Savitsch
lower row: Flossie von Sonklar, Ilse Baravalle, Ilona Bögel, Minni Husemann, Annemarie Donath

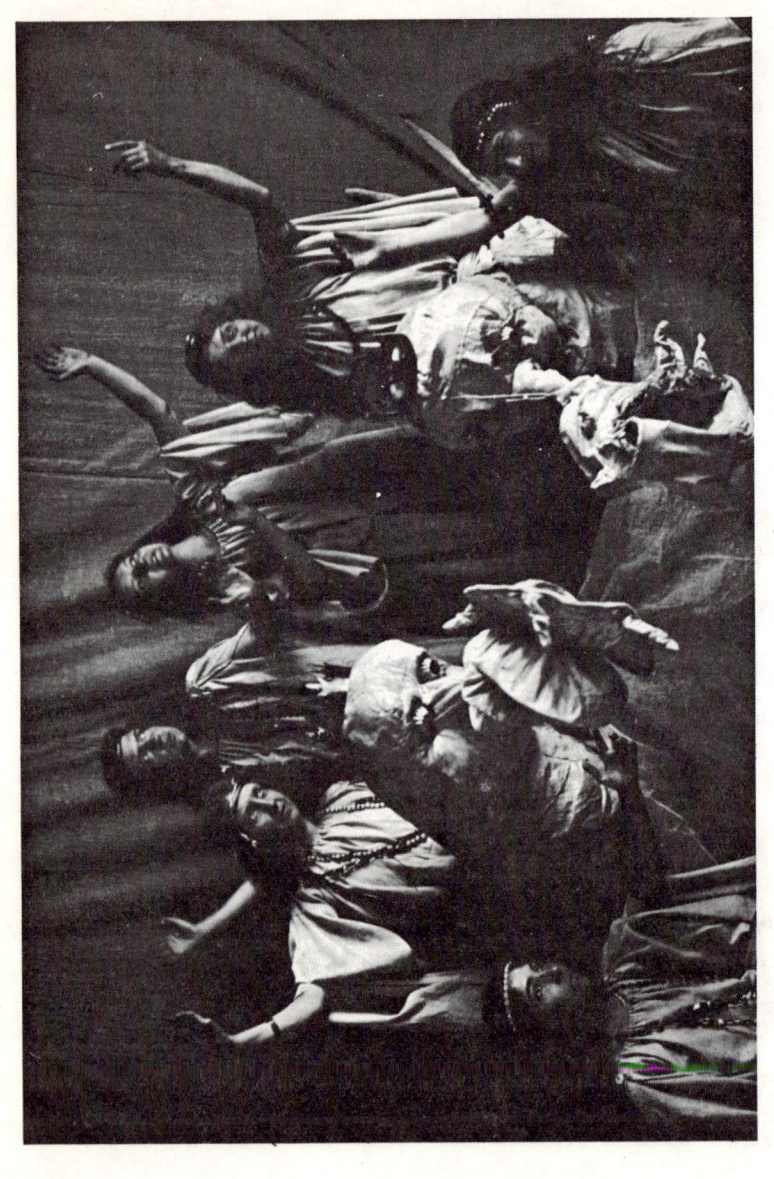

Nereids and Tritons from *Faust* II
upper row, from left to right: Luise Clason, Lisli Dollfus, Annemarie Groh, A. Weyer
lower row: Nora Stein, Minni Husemann

Sirens from *Faust* II
upper row, from left to right: Tatiana Kisseleff, Annemarie Donath
lower row: Agnes Spiller, Edith Röhrle

our muscles would thereby have become hardened and it would have spoiled our eurythmy—quite apart from the fact that we had no time for it. We did the painting of the numbers only during our midday break. How grateful we were to be able to contribute something to the work.

And what can be compared to our feelings when we stood for the first time on the stage of the First Goetheanum! It was inexpressible. Such was the feeling of awe it inspired, one hardly dared breathe. Bathed in sunlight, the colours from the windows played upon the warm wooden pillars, and the colours from the cupolas rayed down from above. I have seen many fine buildings in my time, but there was never anything to compare for wonder and magnificence with the First Goetheanum. It was not only the beauty one experienced, but also the harmony, and one was *forced* to become a different and a better human being when one stood therein; one felt oneself greater, more free and inspired to inner and outer intensive activity. I often spent hours alone in the Goetheanum in order to absorb it all deeply into myself.

I should like to describe an experience to show what effect the Goetheanum had on people. One bright summer's day I was going for a walk with my mother. After a long stroll we came to a part of the hills to the south of the Goetheanum from where one suddenly gets a glimpse of the fairly distant building. It was a wonderful view and we paused to contemplate the sight of the shining building seemingly woven out of gold and silver. The warm light of the wood shone with a golden glow and the domes covered with pale northern slates gleamed silver in the sunlight. At that moment two travelling journeymen came towards us with knapsacks and knotty sticks, almost as in a fairy-tale. They too came to a halt and gazed as if entranced towards the building. One of them said, 'See, it's a real temple! Is it really true? Are there such things?' We told them that we had just come from this 'temple', it was called the 'Goetheanum' and they could go there themselves and even see it from the inside. They stayed with us awhile in devout contemplation and then proceeded on their way towards the Goetheanum.

And now the first rehearsals started in the Goetheanum. The first thing we practised was 'The Twelve Moods' by Rudolf Steiner, to which the music by Jan Stuten was later added. It was so appropriate that the building should be opened with the 'Zodiac'. Eurythmy is a 'dance of the stars' as Rudolf Steiner often called it, for it is born as visible speech out of the interplay of vowels and consonants which come from the planets and the zodiac.

It was not easy at first to get used to the great hall with its slightly sloping stage surrounded by the pillars. The great height, too, threatened us with being 'carried away'. Soon, however, we got accustomed to it and felt quite at home there.

The first event that took place within the Goetheanum commenced with the speech of Hilarius from 'The Guardian of the Threshold', slightly adapted by Rudolf Steiner for the occasion. This was recited by Frau Dr Steiner from the organ gallery. Then Dr Steiner gave an address and the orchestral prelude by Jan Stuten led over into the 'Zodiac', 'The Twelve Moods' by Rudolf Steiner, with which the stage was consecrated.

In later times the performances were so arranged that usually two sections with a serious theme were enacted in the Goetheanum. For the humorous pieces the audience and the stage artists moved to the Workshop for their performance. It would hardly have been possible to have performed humoresques on the Goetheanum stage. The solemn setting would not have allowed the humour to shine through and the character of the pieces would have been lost. The lighting apparatus for eurythmy performances in the First Goetheanum consisted of large wooden trollies placed between the pillars with big coloured light bulbs attached to them. There were also footlights but, of course, no top lights. For the Fairy-tale (*Das Quellenwunder*) from 'The Soul's Probation', we were given a circular raised platform with two steps upon which the 'maidens' could do their movements and under which the 'waterdrops' did theirs.

8. Eurythmy Tours

Eurythmy started to go on tour in 1920. To an ever greater extent it was becoming known to the public. The earliest of the big performances were given in Stuttgart and Zürich. Later came the ones in Essen, Mannheim and the Rhineland. We also repeatedly gave performances at the Group Headquarters in Berlin. In the latter place, among other things, I gave a rather boisterous special number of my own—not, however, quite voluntarily. It happened in the following way. As well as taking part in the eurythmy, I played on the small percussion instruments with the orchestra. The musicians sat in front of the stage at one side. Now at one point, after having finished one of my eurythmy pieces, I had to get changed very quickly, rush across the darkened stage and climb down by the side of the curtain onto a ready positioned chair with the help of one of the musicians. In my haste and in the dark I misjudged my distance and flew through the curtain—which luckily broke my fall—and landed fair and square onto the piano, the percussion instruments *and* onto the musicians. There was a tremendous crash! Fräulein Mitscher, who was attending to the lighting, dared not turn up the lights for a very long time. She had no idea what had happened. When the lights came up again I was sitting on my chair with a very red face and feeling very much ashamed of myself. As I had not hurt myself very much the piece could proceed to the end. Of course everybody, including the audience, was very much shocked and everyone enquired what had happened. Dr Steiner told me afterwards that there need not have been such a rush and it had been arranged for me to creep down very quietly and as far as possible unnoticed. Then we all had a hearty laugh.

The journeys abroad started in 1921—Scandinavia, Czechoslovakia, Austria, Holland, England, etc. Many of the texts were in the language of the country we were visiting, but there were also many German texts, or translations. A new chapter had been opened in the history of eurythmy. For especially characteristic sounds in the languages concerned, Dr Steiner gave new gestures which exactly fitted the nature of the sounds. Also, for the translation of Asiatic languages, he gave characteristic gestures, arm, hand and foot positions and movements which are most interesting and partly very complicated, as for instance in the case of Egyptian, Chinese and Japanese sounds. When we asked him if we could have something for Indian texts too, he said that that was impossible; either we would have to copy Persian miniatures—that might be possible—or we would have to do 'belly dancing' and we would certainly not want to do that.

Travelling in the post-war period of that time was not always easy. The train journeys through Germany in themselves were often hampered by strikes and other technical difficulties and were very long drawn out and strenuous. We arrived in a town, had preliminary practices in order to get familiar with the stage, then dress rehearsals and occasionally gave a performance the same day. Then we travelled to the next town and so on for several weeks on end. It was a tremendously interesting and active time. We were always absorbing new impressions from the countries and peoples we visited. There were always new situations confronting us. Among other things we learned to be mobile in every sense of the word.

Hardly were we back at home than Frau Dr Steiner started to rehearse new programmes with us. I have calculated that in one year I only spent about eight weeks altogether in Dornach. But on our journeyings we saw and experienced so many beautiful things. The time spent in each other's company was so harmonious and we had so much understanding for each other. Each helped the other whenever the opportunity arose. And what fun we had on the long train journeys! Dr Steiner visited the other compartments many times enquiring how we all were, made jokes and encouraged us. On one occasion we arrived in Prague fairly well exhausted after an over-night journey and were received by our hosts and hostesses in the usual way. After a ceremonious greeting the latter wanted to take their guests home with them, but Dr Steiner said, 'Wait a moment, first of all we want to have a good breakfast. I invite you all for that. The eurythmists must discover what a good Bohemian breakfast of coffee and *Kipfeln* [croissants] is like.' So this huge party sat down in the station buffet and enjoyed a very happy and comfortable time together.

While staying in Prague for some time on account of a eurythmy tour and a lecture tour by Dr Steiner, we eurythmists, together with many of the Society members, paid a visit with Herr and Frau Dr Steiner to Karlstein Castle in Bohemia. It is not my task to give the history of this castle. I should only like to draw attention to the wonderful books on the subject: *Karlstein* by Michael Eschborn and *Geistimpulse in der Geschichte des Tschechischen Volkes von den Ursagen bis Karl IV* [Spiritual Impulses in the History of the Czech Peoples from the Time of the Ancient Sagas till that of Charles IV] by Hanna Krämer-Steiner. I can, however, report what Dr Steiner told us on the occasion of this visit.

Of greatest interest to us was the statement that Charles IV was the last emperor to have undergone initiation. The castle was not so much a place for defence and defiance, but was built by the Emperor to house his large collection of antiques and works of art from all over the world. First and foremost he gathered around him persons of high spiritual standing and those who were interested in spiritual matters. The great Chapel of the Holy Cross in all its golden splendour served the inhabitants of the castle and their guests as the service room. For his own private use the Emperor prepared an initiation centre in the main tower to which led a spiral staircase, the walls of which were painted with the story of St Wenzel and the stages of his initiation. Dr Steiner said to us: 'Examine that closely and you will find a great similarity to the account of the *Chemical Wedding of Christian Rosenkreutz*. Later on I heard that Dr Steiner is reported to have said that it *was* the representation of the Chemical Wedding. That is not quite correct for this work came into existence much later. But it is in the same spiritual direction. When one ascends the stairs one comes first of all to the Mary Chapel, on the walls of which are paintings from the Apocalypse. A small door leads along a narrow dark passageway to the Chapel of St Catharine. This was the actual meditation room of the Emperor. He retired into it for longer or shorter periods. His meagre fare was passed to him through a small hole at the base of one of the walls. Above the entrance opposite the altar is the famous double portrait of the Emperor and his wife, Anna von Schweidnitz, who are holding a reliquary cross.

I do not want to forego the account of a charming episode which happened during a visit to that place by Dr Steiner, Frau Dr Steiner and several others. Dr Steiner had once said on a previous occasion that the painters of old, when wishing to differentiate between the ordinary gaze and that of a visionary, depicted the visionary with more or less of a squint. Thus it was quite natural that one of the party should say, on looking at this double portrait: 'Herr Doktor, that must be the gaze of an initiate which you told us about.' Then Dr Steiner smiled and said, 'Look at it more closely, that is not someone squinting but rather someone with a somewhat crafty look. At any rate he seems to be very much in love with her!'

Dr Steiner dearly loved Prague. Time and again he walked through the city and drew the attention of those accompanying him to special objects of interest. He drew particular attention to the connection of the two chapels: the Wenzel Chapel in the Cathedral on the Hradschin and the Chapel of the Holy Cross in Karlstein Castle. It gave him especial pleasure to show us the Goldmaker's Alleyway, where the alchemists used to live in the Middle Ages and which today still exercises such a peculiar charm.

But there were other very exciting journeys I made. First and foremost was the one from Tübingen to Frankfurt, Darmstadt, Baden-Baden and Heidelberg. In Tübingen already there were disturbances among the students, laughter and cat-calls. In spite of that, the performance was carried through to the end and was a great success. In Frankfurt, however, a great commotion broke out among the audience during the first part of the programme, so that we often could hardly understand what Frau Dr Steiner recited from one of the side boxes near the stage. We could not allow any pauses between items, and costume changes had to be carried out with utmost speed. The wardrobe mistresses tore off the used dresses and others held the new ones ready and in no time we were back on the stage again. Amidst whistles and howlings from the gallery we carried through with our performance. Frau Dr Steiner always told us which item came next before we came onto the stage and it happened that she called into the hall: '*Die Klaffer* [The Brawlers], a humorous poem by Goethe.' The audience felt, however, that it was *they* who were referred to and now the uproar broke out in good earnest. When I had a solo piece to perform, the stage manager did not want to let me go onto the stage. 'They will kill you, Missy,' he said, and held me fast. I, however, tore myself free and although I could not hear a note of the music I concluded the number well. The audience in the stalls could not understand what was happening, for most people had nothing against eurythmy and continually kept calling out for those at the back to be quiet. The whole thing was instigated by the radical right-wing opponents, the same who were later to make Dr Steiner's lecture tours in Germany impossible. After changing back into our ordinary clothes we sat in the dressing-room completely exhausted and waited until the crowd had dispersed. Then the police escorted us out of the building by a back exit to our hotel.

Next day there was an early matinée in Darmstadt and this ran perfectly smoothly until the last item. Shortly before this we heard how the gallery doors were flung open and furious cries and cat-calls resounded. The audience called out loudly for silence and we concluded the performance without further hindrance. What had actually happened? The rowdies from Frankfurt had followed us from there, but had been under the impression that the performance was to take place in the afternoon. Thus they arrived too late and of course they were extremely angry. In Baden-Baden, too, it was very uproarious. We were especially fearful for Frau Dr Steiner who sat so near to the audience that she was in great danger. Happily, however, this performance also passed off all right.

9. Actors and Helpers in Dornach

In Dornach at Christmas time the Oberufer Christmas plays were presented—they still are to this day. At that time there were no professional actors in Dornach. Those who were allowed to take part were all amateurs. It was an established tradition for the Schuurman couple to take the parts of the Angel and the Devil, a fact which led one child to ask its parents if Angel and Devil were always married to one another. This gave rise to great merriment in Dr and Frau Dr Steiner and in all of us. Herr Stuten was always Adam in the Paradise play and Fräulein Waller (later Mrs Pyle) was always the Father God. On the other hand, Eve was always chosen afresh every year, as also were the Mary and Joseph of the Shepherds' play.

In my first year in Dornach I was allowed to play the part of the Page in the Three Kings' play, and in 1921 I then played the part of Mary. Already while I was staying in Scandinavia I was busy learning my part for it. Then throughout December the rehearsals took place on the stage in the Workshop in Dornach. For the Paradise and Christmas plays the stage was decked out with fir branches. On the left side of the stage stood a large fir tree which was decorated with oranges and apples for the Paradise play, and with the Christmas tree signs, roses and candles for the Christmas play.

Dr Steiner gave different gestures for the different Maries, for example in the Annunciation scene, the scene with the Shepherds, or with Herod. For me as 'Mary thanking the Shepherds', he prescribed a gesture of blessing, a eurythmical 'D' changing into an 'A'. For

Maria Ina Schuurman
Max Schuurman 20.11.1889–28.2. 1955

Leopold van der Pals
4.7.1884–7.2.1966

Mary's veil he prescribed varying folds, and the style of make-up was differentiated likewise. In the case of one of the Maries, he aimed at a 'Botticelli-like' appearance. With me, he arranged my cloak according to the picture of the *Sistine Madonna* and made me up, even before the first performance, according to this model.

Herr van der Pals, who had composed the music for the plays, took part in them for many years from his vantage point at the piano. At the point in the play where the Star-singer says 'Let's greet our Master . . .' all the players turned and bowed in profound gratitude in the direction of Dr Steiner.

The whole mood of the Christmas plays bore within it something so intimate and radiant that we were all filled with it and upborne by it throughout the Christmas period. Even the smallest parts were enacted with devotion. What a lovely scene was that of the Shepherds or the one where the Angel glided on to the scene illumined in a rosy glow of light to portray the birth of the Christ-child, or the scene where the Kings were dreaming. These plays, collected by Karl Julius Schroer, are written in the Austrian dialect and it was priceless to see how the different actors—mostly foreigners—wrestled with the pronunciation. Dr Steiner articulated most of the sounds, explained the meaning of the words and often acted them himself until the players could succeed in their efforts.

During the first years it was Fräulein Berta Ellram who looked after the costumes. She was a lady from the Baltic who carried out her office with strictness. Together with many other ladies who helped voluntarily, she produced the costumes for the Christmas plays and also for certain scenes from Faust, according to Dr Steiner's instructions. My mother also gave untiring help alongside the work of the carving inside the Goetheanum. The one who contributed most to the store of costumes we acquired was Frau Helene Röchling, the wife of the privy councillor. We called her *Geheimste* [Most Privy] for fun. She effected the purchase of the original store of eurythmy costumes and veils and also helped with the sewing of them. In all things she was untiringly at hand to help whenever she was needed. For many years she accompanied Herr and Frau Dr Steiner on lecture tours. Whenever books worth reading were mentioned in a lecture you could be sure that she would acquire them. In the case of old books long out of print, she did not rest until she had dug them out from somewhere. (Many of these books are still in my possession.) She must have been able to read the wishes of Herr and Frau Dr Steiner in their eyes. To us eurythmists she was the ever helpful mother.

On one occasion, when we had performed the humoresque called *Die Nonnen* [The Nuns] by Christian Morgenstern, she had a marvellous idea. In this poem the nuns have a trunk sent to their nunnery containing a lot of useful and nice objects. On the trunk stands the word 'ESPEDITO', which the nuns make into 'St Expeditus' and revere as a saint. One day, after performing this humoresque, a trunk of this sort appeared in our dressing room. With great glee we unpacked it and found many useful and wished for articles inside. For days Frau 'Geheimrat' Röchling and my mother, who lived together in the same house, had been collecting the things together with a great deal of love and secret enquiries concerning the wishes of individual members of the company.

At quite an early stage, Fräulein Luise Clason, a painter, helped with the costumes and afterwards for several decades she took charge of the wardrobe herself. She was also present on many of our tours. Who could imagine what a deal of work is involved in such a journey lasting weeks! Hundreds of costumes and veils have to be packed and unpacked, pinned and re-pinned, often for different programmes in the same town. Certainly she had help from friends in most of the places where we stopped. Costumes and veils always had to be newly ironed, but most of the work she did herself. In the most tricky and disturbing situations she never got ruffled.

One of the most impressive occasions within the Society was surely the West-East Congress in Vienna in the summer of 1922. In the evenings Dr Steiner held lectures in the great Concert Hall of the Music Society. During the mornings and afternoons there were other lectures and discussions, etc. In addition to that, we gave great public eurythmy performances with a variety of programmes. A breath of happiness pervaded the Congress and every branch of cultural life gained new incentives. On every hand an active social life prevailed among people from every part of the globe. One could see from Dr Steiner's looks that he felt at home in his own country: the openness and liberality of the people all contributed to the festiveness of the occasion. It was to be the last time that we could meet in such harmony and with such joy.

The year 1922 was also the year which saw the birth of the

Christian Community. After Dr Steiner had held his course of lectures for the priests the various services were then held in private for those who were concerned. To that end it was necessary to provide the appropriate vestments. A few days before the services took place Dr Steiner asked Frau Geheimrat Röchling and my mother if they would be willing to undertake this task. And so the two ladies bought the requisite material and then an ardent dressmaking activity began in our house. I was lucky enough to be allowed to help. We worked busily almost day and night, for in a few days everything had to be ready and there were only three of us to do the work. Dr Steiner had asked us to preserve complete silence about the project and so we could not ask anyone to assist us. These days were unforgettable in my mind, it was so wonderful to do our bit in peace and quiet towards the bringing into being of these solemn religious services.

10. The Burning of the First Goetheanum

It was on New Year's Eve of 1922 that the Goetheanum burnt down. Much has been written about it already. I only want to tell of some of the things I personally experienced. On the afternoon of Sunday, 31 December, we had a performance of the first part of 'The Prologue in Heaven' from Part I of *Faust*. In the early morning I had to give a lesson in a small room. Through this fact I passed by the entrance leading to the cellars and heard noises coming from below. I called down to ask if anyone was there, but received no answer. I immediately informed the porter who straightway went to investigate but found nobody there. And when some men made a tour of inspection of the building nothing unusual was discovered. In the First Goetheanum the speaker's desk could be lowered into the stage and in the Faust scene Mephistopheles has to appear at a certain height in this shaft. Because the mechanism always took some time to lower this very large desk, Dr Steiner gave instructions that the process should be set in motion while he was still giving his introductory talk and he would stand more towards the other side of the stage. However, while he was speaking he walked to and fro and did not notice that the shaft was becoming ever deeper and deeper and so he got dangerously near to the edge. Just at the last moment Count Josef Polzer sprang over the footlights, grabbed Dr Steiner's arm and pulled him to safety, otherwise he would have plunged into the depths. That was itself a very frightening beginning.

During the second part we did eurythmy and had to hurry across the stage frequently to make our entrance from the opposite side. This is something we had all done many times before, but on this particular occasion we all felt a kind of dread which was quite inexplicable to us. Exactly in the centre of the east side of the stage there was a fairly deep cavity where later large pieces of scenery could be brought in. It was dark at that point and for the first time we all seemed to get the creeps. I can still recall how I arrived at the other side with beating heart and asked the curtain drawer to see what or who it was that was moving about down there. But here again nothing could be ascertained. During the break Fräulein Waller said to Frau Dr Steiner and to all of us who were gathered there: 'Something awful has happened. My mirror fell from the wall and broke. It's a sign of bad luck.' Frau Doktor turned to her crossly and said, 'But Mita, don't be so silly.' If Fräulein Waller had felt the wall she would probably have noticed that it was warm, because it was just above this place that the fire broke out. After the performance some of the ladies helped Fräulein Clason to put the dresses away. It was then that Frau Schuurman said to me, 'Don't you notice a smell of burning somewhere?' We had a look to see if the irons had been switched off and if everything else was in order, but we could not find anything amiss. And so my mother and I hurried home in order to get a bite to eat before the lecture began. On the way we met Herr O, whose skeleton was later found among the ruins. We said to one another, 'What is *he* doing here at this time?' (He was on his way to the Goetheanum.) He was someone who had always struck us as being a bit uncanny. Later I was called upon to testify in a court of law that I had seen him. He had a crooked spine and was easily recognizable merely on account of his limp, and furthermore he passed by very close to us.

Dr Steiner's lecture was delivered at eight o'clock and afterwards we sat at home to celebrate the coming of the New Year. At that time there were many people lodged with my landlady, Frau Wirz, who lived at what is now the 'Schiefer' boarding house. So there was a large company seated round the table. Suddenly the phone rang. It was Dr Steiner himself who said that we must all come immediately to the Goetheanum, it was on fire and we should bring with us sponges soaked in vinegar. We were up there in a very short time but could not see anything untoward. But then some people emerged from the south doorway and said that the seat of the fire was in what was called the White Room. From this room, in which we often practised, a small door opened into a passageway which led round the building between the two cupolas and gave access to the architraves and cupolas for purposes of repair. If this had been the seat of the fire it was no wonder that the building could not be saved.

We cleared the wardrobes and quite late in the proceedings all of us, namely, all the eurythmists, pulled down the stage curtain. Unfortunately very many valuable instruments and musical scores were destroyed in the organ gallery. The whole of the Workshop was also cleared. The bookshop was emptied of its books by Miss Mackenzie, the librarian, and Günther Schubert, and all of them were taken to the house of de Jaager.

At first a chain of people handed buckets of water from the Workshop to the Goetheanum, but soon it became evident that nothing could be saved by that means. It was also no longer possible to approach too closely to the building. At exactly twelve o'clock—that is, at the moment of New Year—the large cupola burst open and huge flames shot up into the air, sending down showers of sparks in all directions. The fire brigade now concentrated its main effort on saving the Workshop, which they managed to do. Dr Steiner spent most of his time in a little house further down the hill, where he stood at the window until the heat forced him to withdraw.

Towards 7.00 a.m. I and some other people from our house went home to change our clothes (we all looked dreadful) and drink some coffee. We had been helping the whole time wherever possible and now we all felt completely exhausted. The pain was so great that we were unable and unwilling to grasp it. As we came up the hill again we heard Dr Steiner say: 'So terrible, so much work, all destroyed.' I shall never forget his look of sadness! As I was busy cleaning up in the Workshop some time later Dr Steiner approached me and I stood before him with tears in my eyes smiling at him. All I could say was, 'Oh, Herr Doktor.' Further words failed me. I say 'smiling', because at that moment there was the consolation that we still had Dr Steiner! He said to me then, 'Yes, Ilona, we have lost our most beautiful possession, but now we have to work on all the more earnestly!' And thus he presently addressed all the others who were there: 'We shall rebuild. And this evening we shall attempt to perform the Three Kings' play as arranged, however it may turn out.'

There really was no time left for sorrowing. What a lot remained to be done! The Workshop was practically under water, the walls still felt hot and everything was covered in soot! All the scattered objects had to be sought for in the neighbouring houses. Some of them were discovered in the frozen or partly melted slush in the meadows! The great question in everybody's mind was whether it could all be put in order by the afternoon. But the play was actually able to start at 5.00 p.m. Dr Steiner gave an introduction, which touched us all deeply. When Frau Schuurman as the Angel began the greeting and came to the words 'a right good evening, the best of cheer', she was unable to continue. With an indescribably appealing gesture she raised one hand and her head sank down against the staff bearing the star. For seconds she stood thus while a great sob passed through the audience until once more she had taken hold of herself and was able to continue. Herr Aisenpreis, the architect in charge of the building office at the Goetheanum, who like everybody else had been up all night and had suffered rather badly from smoke fumes during the first stages of the fire, was playing the part of Villigrazia. He was so hoarse that he could hardly utter a word, but that did not particularly disturb anyone.

During the performance watchers stood in readiness with buckets of water in and around the Workshop in case the building, which was still hot, should break into flames. That same evening Dr Steiner continued the lecture cycle he had already begun. It was an unbelievable achievement without parallel. Who in the world could have done the same?

Frau Dr Steiner, who had remained in Haus Hansi during the fire and had kept herself informed of events, had suffered immensely. How courageously she had been able to suppress her own feelings in order to stand strongly at the side of Dr Steiner. All who had experienced the fire felt that it was something more than just losing a dear friend. For us the Goetheanum was our true home. Every detail had been worked upon with love and devotion, most of it at the hands of artists. During the war years people of seventeen different nationalities had worked together in friendship and harmony with one another.

Certainly work was soon to start on the building of the Second Goetheanum, but no comparison can be made between them. What a kind destiny it was which had allowed us to experience the First Goetheanum! I may here add that Dr Steiner never allowed us to speak of the 'Old Goetheanum'. It was always to be the First Goetheanum and the Second Goetheanum.

11. Reverence Towards the Goetheanum

The rehearsals we had on the stage of the First Goetheanum often lasted a very long time. At the base of the pillars were the carved thrones, upon which no one would ever have thought of sitting. One day, however, I put my little gold watch on a ledge at the back of one of these thrones where it was joined to the pillar. It was a little niche in which I could feel confident it would be safe during the rehearsal at which I did not wish to wear it. The place where I had hidden it was not visible from the auditorium. When Dr Steiner passed by on his way to explain something to us, he saw the watch lying there and asked: 'To whom does this watch belong?' I came forward immediately and he said to me, 'I should not have thought it possible that anyone would have dreamed of putting anything on these thrones.' When I explained that I had only put it right at the back, he said: 'Even there nothing should be placed, it is quite out of the question, just think about it!' All the eurythmists, including myself, were very concerned and it was a good lesson to us.

A similar event occurred in the large auditorium during a rehearsal when another eurythmist was eating a dry bun behind a pillar near the west entrance. That, too, was seen by Dr Steiner who called her to him and said, 'If you want to eat then do so in the dressing room or in the lobbies, but never in the hall. Don't you see that it is something quite impermissible? It simply mustn't be done!'

On another occasion, when he saw a couple of young people sitting on the balustrade of the terrace, he ordered them to come down immediately and said it was bad manners to behave like that in the building. He never allowed anyone to enter the Goetheanum without stockings, and a woman in trousers who wished to enter was firmly but politely denied access. (At that time a lady in trousers was a very rare sight.) Men not wearing jackets were also not welcome there—they would not go to a concert so sloppily dressed! 'You would not enter a church like that,' said Dr Steiner. Many years later when I told a young pupil about this she said: 'But the Goetheanum is not a church.' 'No,' I replied, 'it is *much, much more!*'

Even the Dutch Prince Consort of that time who came to visit the Goetheanum was exhorted by Dr Steainer: 'Your Majesty will excuse me, but one may not enter the building with a cigar.' And His Majesty begged Dr Steiner's pardon and left his cigar outside! Perhaps it would be appropriate to apply Dr Steiner's rules at the present day, which is so lacking in any feeling of reverence.

After the fire all events took place in the Workshop once more. How difficult and painful it was to accustom ourselves again to such restricted space—and yet how thankful we were that this was still left us. The most impressive item from the first eurythmy programme after the fire was the presentation of the Chorus of Spirits from the first part of *Faust*: 'Woe! Woe! Thou hast it destroyed, the beautiful world!' The great sorrow we endured through the loss of the Goetheanum might have depressed us sorely, but it was once more Dr and Frau Dr Steiner who summoned us and urged us on to still more intensive work through their unparalleled example.

12. Dr Steiner's Illness and Death

From 1924 onwards Dr Steiner's health started to deteriorate. In spite of this he got through a tremendous amount of work. He held lectures and lecture courses in Stuttgart, Prague and Paris and, of course, in Dornach alongside negotiations, discussions, interviews and work connected with the building of the Second Goetheanum.

There was an agricultural course, a medical course, a course for tone eurythmy and, later, the pedagogical course and the course for speech eurythmy. There followed lectures in Torquay and London. At the beginning of September there were more lectures in Dornach, among which was the drama course from 15–23 September and a course for the priests. Dr Steiner often gave two or three lectures in one day. With a final summoning of his forces he succeeded in achieving all that. Frau Dr Steiner was constantly concerned about his health. I still remember the lecture which he gave, about the middle of September, when one could see by his looks as he walked to the speaker's desk that he was not feeling well. And on that occasion he really did have to break off his lecture and could only continue after a short pause.

He gave an address on 28 September which deeply moved his audience, not only on account of its mighty content but also because we all felt the question rising up within us: How long shall we still have Dr Steiner here among us? It was really the last address he gave. From that day onwards he was confined to his bed. He lay in his Studio in the Workshop. But even from his bed of sickness he wrote articles and held talks on the most varied aspects of the work with those whom it concerned. I was still able to speak with him about a matter connected with eurythmy. He himself certainly believed that he still had a long time ahead of him for work, and even four days before his death he asked Herr Aisenpreis to come to him to discuss the new building plans.

And so 30 March 1925 arrived. A telephone call came from the Workshop in the early morning asking me to come immediately. I already had an inkling that something awful must have happened. When I arrived at the gate to the building site I heard the children who were taught in the now no longer existing building office romping about on the playground and I thought with relief that it could not be so bad after all. But at that moment Fräulein Mitscher came out of the Workshop and asked the children to be quiet. Then she came up to me and said, 'Dr Steiner is dead.' 'No—oh, no,' I said. But she merely made a helpless gesture as her voice failed her. I then accompanied her to the door of the Workshop, where the news was once more confirmed. Thereupon I hurried home to convey the sad news to my family. We then immediately went up the hill once more, Frau Geheimrat Röchling, my mother and I, and my husband,

and were allowed into the Studio. Dr Steiner lay in bed at the foot of the Christ statue which he himself had carved. His features, which had mostly showed signs of pain during recent times, were now rejuvenated and of immense grandeur and permeated at the same time with a touching mildness. Gradually more people arrived to see Dr Steiner once more. And I went again and again to the Studio on this and on succeeding days.

Frau Dr Steiner, who was in Stuttgart with a group of eurythmists at the time, was informed of Dr Steiner's worsening condition on Sunday, 29 March after ten o'clock at night and again on Monday morning, 30 March after six o'clock. Immediately after Dr Steiner's death Frau Dr Steiner was informed by telephone and she arrived by midday in Dornach and drove directly to the Workshop, where she then remained alone for several hours. For the lying-in-state which was to take place on the evening before the cremation, we eurythmists, together with others, decorated the black-hung stage with fir branches, foliage and an endless number of flowers. In order to make room for the exceedingly large gathering of visitors the walls separating this from the machine-room had been removed and the doors leading to the practice rooms had been left open. Dr Steiner lay in state in the middle of the stage, the priests stood around the coffin and on all four sides of it stood large lighted candles. The whole ceremony, which concluded with music by Jan Stuten and an impressive obituary speech by Albert Steffen, was something which could not easily be forgotten by those who were privileged to take part in it. A solemn stillness hovered in the room. With a deep sense of mourning, but likewise with unlimited gratitude and love in their hearts, those who were present raised up their thoughts to their great leader and teacher.

On the following afternoon, April 3 (which is the historic Good Friday), the cremation took place at the old crematorium in Basel, celebrated with the ritual of the Christian Community by Dr Rittelmeyer. A vast crowd had gathered which could not be encompassed within the small funeral hall, so most of the people stood outside in the open air. I too was among the latter and could only take part in the service from a distance. My participation was none the less deep for that, however. A clear blue sky and radiant sunshine, the singing of birds in the newly stirring springtime—there was a Good Friday magic in the air as in Wagner's *Parsifal*, which united all of us, both those within and without, through the knowledge that we were rendering homage to one who was among the greatest of humankind in whose earthly activity we had been privileged to share.

* * *

Since Dr Steiner's death the question has often been asked as to whether there is any truth in the rumour that he had been poisoned. Up till now the question always came from the circle of the Members, but lately a man from the public, a journalist, raised the same question with me, but in such a way that I had to conclude that he had already been told a great deal about it which was inaccurate or misleading. Over the years I have kept silent about all the things of which I have personal knowledge. Now, however, I feel it incumbent upon me to counter these rumours with what I know from my own experience.

On the occasion of the evening party during the Christmas gathering on New Year's Day 1924, several of the eurythmists were serving the guests who sat at small tables in the large hall of the Workshop. From the large room a passageway led past the stage to the dressing rooms. In one of these rooms a tea-kitchen had been set up and from there we carried tea, coffee and cakes to the guests. As I happened to be walking along this passage with a cup of tea, the curtain separating it from the rest of the hall parted and Dr Steiner came staggering towards me, snow-white and groaning loudly. I quickly put the cup down and was just able to guide him to a chair. All he said was: 'I feel so poorly.' I wanted to go quickly to fetch Frau Dr Steiner and Frau Dr Wegman, but he held my hand firmly and said, 'No, stay with me—water please, water.' Fräulein Mitscher, who just then appeared, ran for the water but I could not go away because my arm was supporting Dr Steiner. He emptied the glass which Fräulein Mitscher gave him. We asked him what had happened and he said, 'I have been poisoned.'

One could see that he was in terrible pain. He was icy cold and bathed in sweat. Fräulein Mitscher and Frau Turgenieff, who had also arrived, and I decided to go and fetch help. Then Frau Dr Steiner came from the hall and asked, 'Has something happened?' When she saw Herr Doktor lying there in the chair she went up to him and asked again, 'What has happened?' Dr Steiner told her too: 'I have been poisoned—how are the other Members of the Vorstand?' Frau Dr told him that they were all happily chatting. Only she had felt uneasy at his long absence. We then brought Dr Steiner with great difficulty to his room and bedded him down on the sofa. Then Frau Turgenieff went to fetch Frau Dr Wegman. Fräulein Mitscher, Frau Turgenieff and I waited by the door for news of him. After a while Frau Doktor appeared and said that Dr Steiner wanted us to say nothing about it to anyone. Dr Steiner was then taken home to Villa Hansi and after medical attention and a milk-cure he recovered.

Until his death in March 1925, that is to say, till long after the tea-party, he did a tremendous amount of work and went on lecture tours, so that one cannot say that he died from poison. The cause of death according to the doctor's certificate was something quite different, but it is also true that from that time onwards he was never in quite such good health. As often and as intensively as Fräulein Mitscher, Frau Turgenieff and I have pondered about what happened at the tea-party; there was never a solution to this riddle.

13. The Work of Frau Dr Steiner After Dr Steiner's Death

I should like to describe the time after Dr Steiner's death only briefly. In the first place there was the great work that Frau Dr Steiner achieved in producing the whole of the Mystery Drama cycle, the staging of *Faust* Parts I and II for the Second Goetheanum stage, the Schiller plays and the great Steffen plays. Each of these was an enormous task on its own and alongside that there were the great eurythmy performances. While Dr Steiner was alive only single scenes of *Faust* had been performed in the Workshop under his direction. How marvellous it was to see how Frau Dr Steiner developed what he had given, adapted it to the new conditions and was intent on drawing the best out of every single scene. If something did not turn out according to her wishes the scene was practised over and over again, and occasionally she came onto the stage herself and recited it for us. Her often only lightly delineated presentations of Manto, Erichto or Helen were unique experiences. With what strength and ability of expression she portrayed such characters!

Frau Dr Steiner also worked intensively to mould and transform some of the eurythmy items. A specially noteworthy achievement among many others was the work she did on the Goethe poem *An den Mond* [To the Moon], *Füllest wieder Busch und Tal* . . . [Bush and vale thou fillst once more. . .]. To this poem there was a very simple form given by Dr Steiner which, if not very well performed, could be very monotonous. Though the eurythmists had worked very well at this poem on that occasion Frau Dr Steiner was not at all satisfied with it and found it 'terribly boring'. And now she showed how one could arrive at the right style for a poem of this kind. It was not enough to make 'beautiful' sounds and forms, but the whole human being must be involved in it. The timing and intensity of sound and, in particular, the rhythm had to be finely attuned and differentiated. Whether the foot was set down carefully and sensitively or with a firm tread, and whether the movements were to be made large or small, all this had to be penetrated by feeling, and thought through in advance. And, above all, it had to become *experience*. Thus Frau Dr Steiner worked it through stanza by stanza until at length it took on a quite different appearance. I have never seen this poem done with such perfection since.

When I took this poem with my class recently the children said to me, 'Oh, that boring thing.' Then I spoke to them about what happened at that time and asked them if they would not try it once more and then, if they still did not like it, they might drop it. In the end they did not want to stop practising it, and it became one of their favourite pieces. They never said afterwards that it was a boring poem.

In the case of humoresques, too, Frau Dr Steiner did not want any frippery. 'Work out of the sound, otherwise it will just be mimicry and that is dilettantism.' In connection with humoresques, I too had a nice experience similar to the one just mentioned. During a course for 'older' ladies I suggested to them that they might like to try a humoresque. Most of them were quite shocked and said that that was not in their line, they would feel 'silly' if they tried to be humorous. Thereupon I explained to them that they did not have to be humorous themselves—indeed, it was forbidden them—and I promised them that they would gradually get a great deal of pleasure out of it, but that they would have to work very hard and take into consideration much more than just the forming of sounds. It then became a really pleasurable undertaking and the dear ladies did not feel a bit 'silly' during the process.

Thus was demonstrated in the teaching of eurythmy what Frau Dr Steiner called 'working with the sound *and* with the meaning'—working out of the *spirit* of a thing! She once took the Goethe poem *Wanderers Sturmlied* [Traveller's Storm-song] with us. There are many Greek names in this poem and Frau Dr Steiner now put the whole circle of eurythmists, both those engaged in the poem and others sitting in the hall, to the test. 'What is the "mud" of Deucalion's deluge? What is the Castalian Fountain? Who is Pythius Apollo? Who are Father Bromius and Jupiter Pluvius? What do you know about Anacreon? About Theocritis?' and so on. We were greatly relieved by the fact that most of the answers could be supplied by one of the youngest eurythmists who had just left the Waldorf School. Frau Dr Steiner said to us: 'How do you expect to present a poem in the right way if the names, vicinity and date to which it refers are of no significance to you and you do not know anything about them? Without comprehensive knowledge there is no true art and especially not in eurythmy.' How emphatic she was that we should be able to discriminate between a poem by Goethe, Nietzsche, Heine and so on, and that only by concerning ourselves with the relevant poet or musician could we acquire the right style.

The same thing as that pertaining to *Wanderers Sturmlied* held good for *Der Ritt in den Tod* [The Ride into Death] by Conrad Ferdinand Meyer. Also in that case the historical background should be known. Yes, and how she loved 'Cordinand', as she called Conrad Ferdinand Meyer, and loved to recite his poems! What a wealth of lecture themes she developed. Whether they were short, delicate, lyrical poems, or solemn majestical ones, or even dramatic pieces, she always gave them fresh shades of meaning. It was unforgettable for me—and surely for many of my colleagues too—how Frau Dr Steiner recited from *Iphigenia*. *Und an dem Ufer steh ich lange Tage, das Land der Griechen mit der Seele suchend.* [And many days I stand beside the shore, seeking with my soul the land of Greece.] Or how beautiful it was to observe how she lived inwardly with a poem. I have often sat with bated breath so as not to miss a single word of it.

And when she recited for eurythmy one felt oneself carried along with her. A pause she made could take one away as if on wings. How grand was her capacity for enthusiasm. She simply swept one off one's feet and drew one along with her. She was our continual spur and always asked from us more than we thought ourselves capable, so that we had to make a tremendous effort to meet her demands.

The work was certainly not always easy, but equally certainly it was to our good when we did not give in. Today, after nearly 60 years of my eurythmy career, I can affirm that I learned most of all from those moments of greatest difficulty when I had to exert myself most for my objective. Thus it is in the whole of life, and because art has to be true experience one has to struggle with it in order to reproduce it in all its perfection.

I should now like to add something to the foregoing which is not, or is *no longer*, generally known. Many years ago we wanted to give Frau Dr Steiner a pleasant surprise on her birthday by practising *Die Geheimnisse* [The Mysteries] by Goethe. We spoke to Dr Steiner about our intention, but he said we should abandon this idea as this poem was not suitable for being performed in eurythmy. So we had to relinquish our cherished plan. And the same thing happened with the 'Dedication' from *Faust*. About the latter Dr Steiner also said that it would be impossible to portray it in eurythmy, it could only be presented through the spoken word. I feel obliged to say this here, because such things as this easily become forgotten.

This statement by Rudolf Steiner is not just applicable to the time it was spoken, but it still holds good today.

14. Experiences at the Theatre

To go with Dr Steiner to the theatre was a quite special experience. Once when Frau Dr Steiner had invited me to lunch I was asked by Dr Steiner if I knew the *Meistersinger* and whether I would like to see it with him that evening. Of course I was delighted and joyfully accepted his invitation. A telephone call was made to the box office then and there and luckily there were still tickets to be had. After the meal, over a cup of black coffee, Dr Steiner suddenly said, 'Well, that's it then! I can't go to the theatre.' My face grew very long and I was nearly in tears, as Dr Steiner repeated his statement with great emphasis: 'That's it, I am unable to go.' Evidently he was waiting for somebody to ask him why he could not go and at last it was Frau Dr Steiner who said to him, 'Is it quite impossible for you to go? Have you got something else on which is very important?' At last, with a sly smile in my direction, he answered, 'I haven't got a decent tie to put on and I can't be seen with Ilona in this old thing.' How we all laughed! Frau Doktor had of course noticed that Dr Steiner was pulling our legs, but nevertheless someone ran out and bought him a new cravat.

So that evening a large party assembled at the theatre and Dr Steiner said, 'But I have to sit next to Ilona to explain things to her.' Thus I was allowed to sit next to Dr Steiner and every now and again I received a little nudge which meant that I was to pay special heed. At the scene where Stolzing is about to stroll down the street Dr Steiner said (not exactly quietly), 'Here he comes, here he comes.' It was obviously delighting him, but his neighbours called out 'pst' and he whispered to me, 'We've got to be quiet.' *I* had not uttered a word! He laughed as I have hardly ever seen anyone laugh at the scene with Beckmeister and where the scuffle takes place and was evidently enjoying himself to the full. During the break he explained to us that it should have been an elder tree by the house of Hans Sachs, even though Sachs sings about a *Flieder* [lilac]. At St John's tide there are no lilac bushes in bloom any more and in some districts *Hollunder* [elder] is called *Flieder*.

On another occasion when I was with Dr Steiner at the theatre it was *Parsifal* we saw. Dr Steiner gave us various explanations. He told us that Amfortas should be wearing a red head-band, not because of a wound there but to show his rank of initiation. In the same way Klingsor should wear a large pair of spectacles to indicate that he is a black magician who sees everything distorted through a mirror or through glasses. All instructions and stage directions that Wagner gave have to be taken seriously if his operas are to produce the right effect. Thus in the scene where the Grail Knights greet each other Wagner has specified a *Nachziehschritt* [a step in which the feet are brought together between every forward pace]. It would then become a kind of threefold stepping as in eurythmy, carried out in 4/

4 time. That would be easy to do—I have tried it out several times. The singers are afraid of that, firstly because they think they might not arrive in time at their alotted place on the stage and secondly because they probably do not know that this is also part of the ritual. If it were done in this way the greeting itself would not appear so clumsy and self-conscious. The 'Evoe' which we do in eurythmy would be most suitable on this occasion. If it were properly practised the actors would certainly find great satisfaction in it.

I once spoke about it to someone who had the role of Parsifal. He was an Anthroposophist and became very enthusiastic about what I told him. He did his best to follow these instructions or have them carried out in this way. That was in a performance of *Parsifal* in Mannheim under the directorship of Wilhelm Furtwängler. It had a specially festive character. Frau Geheimrat Röchling donated some special stage properties and costumes and also had special stage curtains made for it. Everything was faithfully copied according to the performances in Bayreuth, just as Wagner had instructed. The conductor and the singers were very enthusiastic about it and gave of their best. It interested them to be able to take part in something which went beyond the usual run of things. Furtwängler, who knew a lot about Anthroposophy, was very glad to be able to awaken an understanding for such things in his companions through his knowledge of the spiritual background. He was thus able to rouse them to more intensive and enjoyable participation. It was a truly festive and solemn performance which was received with interest and acclaim far beyond the borders of the town itself.

At the Festival plays in Bayreuth where I have seen *Parsifal* several times—also during the lifetime of Cosima Wagner, who granted me an audience—the instructions of Wagner were, of course, strictly adhered to. At certain particular passages of the music Dr Steiner said to me that this was directly inspired by the Holy Grail, that is to say, divinely inspired. When I went to *Parsifal* with Dr Steiner he said to me beforehand: 'I will give you discreet signals when these passages occur and then you will be able to pay particular attention.' To my great delight these were just the passages I particularly loved.*

---

* Those are the last twenty bars of the Prelude and the passage during the Good Friday enchantment scene which accompanies the words 'Nature her innocence has won, all is renewed once more this day'.

Following on from my account of the experiences I had with Dr Steiner at the *Parsifal* performances, I should like to relate further the conversation we had on another occasion about Parzival. He then told us that the instructions given to Parzival by Trevrizent as described by Wolfram von Eschenbach took place in the vicinity of the Eremitage in Arlesheim. He indicated the place rather exactly, namely, where the Hermit's Hut stands today. I can remember that in my youth its appearance was slightly different. It was a small, longish site, with a little stream flowing past it which descended from the rocks above. There it was that many serious conversations must have taken place between these two. Dr Steiner described the whole vicinity as 'Grail territory'. Parzival actually received his initiation after long years of searching for the Grail Castle, wandering through ever-changing scenery, through forests, over mountains, past still lakes and beside flowing rivers where the whole elemental world spoke to him—a kind of initiation through the world of nature—till, after he had gained maturity, he came to King Amfortas one Good Friday to be made the King of the Grail.

It is probable that there were several castles where people lived who belonged to the Grail Community; perhaps these castles were built of wood and have later disintegrated or have been destroyed. Thus it may be presumed that in the vicinity of Trevrizent's dwelling in Arlesheim such a castle as this once stood. Dr Steiner said that the Grail Castle of which Titurel and Amfortas were the Guardians was in northern Spain and later was at Montségur in south-west France. He added: 'If you draw a diagonal from the present-day rock-encircled monastery of San Juan de la Peña as far north-eastwards towards Montségur in France as San Juan de la Peña lies south-westwards [from the French border?], then you will find the first two Grail Castles.' One must not forget that the Grail events at Montségur happened during the ninth and tenth centuries, and that the Cathars lived there and perished on the funeral pyre during the twelfth century. The two currents are not interconnected.

At this point it ought to be recounted that Dr Steiner confirmed the truth of the legend that St Odile in her flight from her pursuing father took refuge in the rocky cleft of the Hohlefelsen [Hollow Rocks], sometimes called the Orilusfelsen [Orilus Rocks] which lie near to Castle Birseck in Arlesheim.

And here I might also be allowed to relate an experience of mine

The 'hermit's hut' in the Ermitage, Arlesheim,
In this vicinity Trevrizent's instruction of Parzival took place

The Ermitage in Arlesheim

which goes to show how very special circumstances connect me with the Wagner family. I was about four or five years old when my parents were staying on the Bürgerstock mountain. After lunch I was always put to bed and was supposed to go to sleep. One day, however, I got out of bed and escaped onto the street unnoticed. I ran hither and thither to look at the world for myself quite alone. All I can remember of it now is that I was suddenly seized from behind and someone cried out, 'Stop, young lady, you can't go down there!' My struggles were of no avail. A large stranger carried me back to the hotel in his arms and deposited me with my parents, who were not a little horror-struck to hear from the gentleman that he had saved me at the last moment from falling over the precipice. One second later and I would have been irrevocably lost. When I was grown up I was told that this gentleman was none other than Siegfried Wagner. When I told Dr Steiner about this incident he remarked, 'Yes, you have a special connection with the Wagner family.' Many years later, while attending the Festival plays in Bayreuth, I paid a visit to Haus Wahnfried and took the opportunity of thanking Siegfried Wagner for having saved my life. He remembered the occasion straight away and said: 'Was it you then? My knees still tremble today when I think about it, and for a long time I was not able to forget those moments of terror. How lucky that I was near at hand and was able to do something about it.' The memory of it was so vivid to him that he shook me by the hand over and over again.

I was at the theatre with Dr Steiner on another occasion. It was a most amusing episode. *Die Fledermaus* was being performed in Mannheim which we heard of while we were sitting at lunch— rather like on the previous occasion in Stuttgart. Dr Steiner was enthusiastic about it straight away and suggested that we should all go to see it. He even started to hum some of the tunes and said, 'Are you as fond of *Die Fledermaus* as I am?' Whereupon I answered that I did not know it, for at that time I felt myself far too superior to go to an operetta! But Dr Steiner was of the opinion that one simply has to know it—'It is a classical piece of music.' So again there was a large party assembled that evening in the theatre and we were all very happy. The one who enjoyed himself most was probably Dr Steiner. His Viennese nature with its familiarity with and love of the Strauss waltzes came to the fore. And how well he knew his Strauss! During the intervals he prepared us for the humorous bits that were

Rock fissure in the Hohlefelsen near Arlesheim,
where St Odile took refuge

Cave in fissure of the Hohlefelsen
into which a person of medium height would fit

to come and I noticed that during the performance he occasionally looked our way to study our reactions. When we then practised the humoresque *Die Fledermaus* by Christian Morgenstern he wanted a few bars of the operetta to be played before it started. Frau Dr Steiner thought that inappropriate, but Dr Steiner said to her 'Why not?' and sang a few bars in a loud voice. We, of course, thought that was wonderful, and thus it came about and was ever afterwards done that way. First a few bars of the music were played and then, on the last note, Fräulein von Baravalle sprang onto the stage as the Strauss 'Bat' and I was supposed to represent the animal 'bat'. Frau Doktor also enjoyed it very much herself.

15. Remarks by Dr Steiner About Various Pictures

The Picture of Brother Mark

Frau Helene Röchling asked Dr Steiner to give her the subject for an ex-libris and he suggested that she should take a motif from the poem *Die Geheimnisse* [The Mysteries] by Goethe, the scene where Brother Mark stands in contemplation of the pentagram [the Rosy Cross, surely?] at the entrance to the temple (or monastery). Hermann Linde made a painting of it which portrayed the west entrance of the First Goetheanum in front of which stands the monk. Dr Steiner himself added the flowers to right and left. On that occasion Hermann Ranzenberger stood as model for 'Brother Mark'. This picture was later transferred to a copper plate. To begin with Frau Röchling had it in our flat in Dornach and later took it with her to Germany. The house where she lived and where the picture was kept was destroyed during the Second World War. Only very few things were preserved, but this was one of them.

Shortly after Frau Röchling died her daughter wrote to me that she did not know what to do with it and would I like to have it. I accepted her offer with great pleasure and she sent it off to me immediately. Some time later a message came from the Basel Badischer railway station that a picture had arrived for me and that

Brother Mark
Copper plate engraving of a picture by Hermann Linde

I was to collect it. After searching for a long time in the various offices I finally came upon it tucked away in a corner under a lot of clutter, without any packing and with the frame broken and still containing pieces of the broken glass. I took it to the customs officer who looked at it in disgust and then decided that it was an oil-painting and therefore would cost several hundred francs. I explained to him that the picture had been painted in Dornach and that one could see that it was a picture of the First Goetheanum. He very impolitely declared that he knew nothing of that and if I could not prove that it came from Dornach I would have to pay duty on it. That made me very unhappy, for how could I afford that amount and how was I to find a proof of its origin? Just as I was about to despair an elderly porter came that way with a lamp almost like the man in Goethe's *Fairy-tale*. He gave a start when he saw the picture and called out with glee: 'Ah, how nice, that is the First Goetheanum. That was such a wonderful building and it is a great shame that it was burned down.' The customs officer asked: 'Do you know that picture, then?' And the elderly man answered: 'Of course I know it. I worked in Dornach for many years and Dr Steiner was such a kind man, he gave me and so many others so much advice and help. I shall never forget him!'

The customs officer was noticeably impressed by this and said to me, 'Well, if that's the case then you may take your picture with you.' How grateful I was to the elderly man! We shook hands like long lost friends. He did not want to accept anything from me and said how happy he was to have been able to help. So I went home with my precious picture—and there it still hangs to this day, newly cleaned and framed, and the cause of much pleasure and amazement to all who visit me.

The Pictures of Goethe's Fairy-tale

I am delighted to comply with Agnes Linde's request to relate the history of how the pictures of Goethe's *Fairy-tale* came to be painted.

In 1917 the Second Group of the General Anthroposophical Society in Mannheim was founded by Helene Röchling and my mother, Erna Bögel, in our house. On the lower floor were large banqueting rooms suitable for Group meetings. In the first place the walls, which until then had been hung with large oil-paintings of landscapes and so on, had to be redecorated with pictures of a more meaningful kind. Dr Steiner was asked for his advice and he suggested that we should ask one of the most accomplished painters in Dornach, Hermann Linde, to paint a series of pictures from Goeth's *Fairy-tale of the Green Snake and the Beautiful Lily* and from the Mystery Drama, 'The Portal of Initiation'. He pointed out that these great Imaginations were particularly suitable for the adornment of rooms for Anthroposophical activities. In his Dornach lecture of 8 July 1924, Dr Steiner speaks about the connection between the *Fairy-tale* of Goethe and 'The Portal of Initiation'.

Hermann Linde became enthusiastic straight away. After a few preliminary consultations, mainly concerning the number and size of the pictures, he set to work to make sketches and diagrams. These all still exist and are works of art in themselves.

After the completion of this basic work the actual painting could begin. This was in the autumn of 1919. What was called the Linde-Studio was situated in the grounds of the Goetheanum and it was here that Hermann Linde worked every day. Here he could apply all his rich experience acquired through his painting in the large cupola of the First Goetheanum. Dr Steiner visited him nearly every morning to see how the work was progressing and to give new encouragement and advice both as to the content and the technique. Frau Röchling, my mother and I were often asked to be present with him. It was very enjoyable to watch quietly how a great work of art comes into being, to experience the devotion and gratitude with which Hermann Linde listened to the instructions of Dr Steiner and also to see with what pleasure and understanding Dr Steiner entered into the special nature of the task by always coming up with new suggestions. Often, after having watched silently for a longer period, he would take the brush himself to lighten where it was too dark or add a few strokes somewhere else and it could also happen that he just painted with the brush in the air. Hermann Linde watched carefully and immediately understood what Dr Steiner meant and then transferred it to the canvas. Both of them derived great pleasure from doing this work together. Afterwards Hermann Linde loved to tell us how fortunate he had been—and how wonderful it must be for us and the group— that the work of Dr Steiner's spirit and of his hands was visibly enshrined in these pictures.

Owing to war conditions the pictures never reached our house in Mannheim. At first this made us very sad, but outer circumstances made insurmountable difficulties for us. Later events proved that it had been a stroke of good fortune because the house was completely destroyed during the Second World War. After these twelve large pictures had been in our Dornach apartments for many years they once more came into the possession of Agnes Linde. They have also been displayed in exhibitions in the Goetheanum, for instance, when Dr Steiner exhibited them in the White Room of the First Goetheanum during his lecture-cycle given to teachers from England at Christmas 1921. Hilde Boos-Hamburger wrote a very nice article that appeared in the newsletter *Das Goetheanum* (24 January 1937) about the life and work of Hermann Linde, with especial reference to his pictures of *The Fairy-tale of the Green Snake and the Beautiful Lily*.

Notes by the Painter Wilhelm Nedella about the 'Druid Picture' after a discussion about it with Rudolf Steiner

These notes from the estate of Wilhelm Nedella, who worked for many years in the Goetheanum, have come into my hands. They were written by him after a discussion on the subject with Rudolf Steiner. They should not be lost because there are not many comments made by Rudolf Steiner about his own pictures and sketches.

[For the following notes I have made use of the translation by Janet Currie for the *Anthroposophical Quarterly*, Winter 1961. Translator.]

What strikes one immediately in this picture is the powerful and yet so simple composition which consciously and artistically brings into antithesis the polarities of colour and contents, and arouses an inner tension in the soul of the beholder. If one looks first at the diagonal *a* to *b* in the picture, one perceives the division of the dark earthly masses in blue, from the air–light–warmth cosmic element in yellow, which, in the upper right-hand corner, rises to the uttermost light pole (the sun). Below, on the left edge opposite in extreme contrast, is the dead black formation which bears the blue rock. On the other hand, if one looks at the diagonal *c–d* in the picture, then up on the left one has the Druid priest standing erect by the three altars surrendering his whole being to the sun-filled cosmos, the highest artistry of which man is capable—conscious communion with the gods, an act of worship which only an initiate can perform. At the bottom right-hand corner again, there is the figure of a woman sitting shelling beans or perhaps even mending fishing nets—a simple, uninitiated being absorbed in an occupation which belongs completely to the earth, to a lower order of things. 'Here we have the beloved earth,' said the teacher. Behind the woman rise cone-shaped forms in light blue, and it is immaterial whether one takes these as indicating the homes of the primitive people of that time or as fishing nets spread out to dry (for these people were fishers). Still higher up on a sloping declivity is still another altar stone. No Druid stands on it but a gigantic elemental being—shown as a giant formed of mist—(significantly, in brown like the clouds of mist indicated in this region at the edge) a being which is placing its arm (half-hoof, half-claw) on the abandoned altar to take possession of it. It must be stated here that when old mystery or cult centres are abandoned, neglected and no longer regularly used, they become a magical focal point for these lower, earth-bound, elementals of the powers of Nature, Snow, Frost and Storm, who greedily absorb the spirituality which still clings to these places and simply take possession of them.

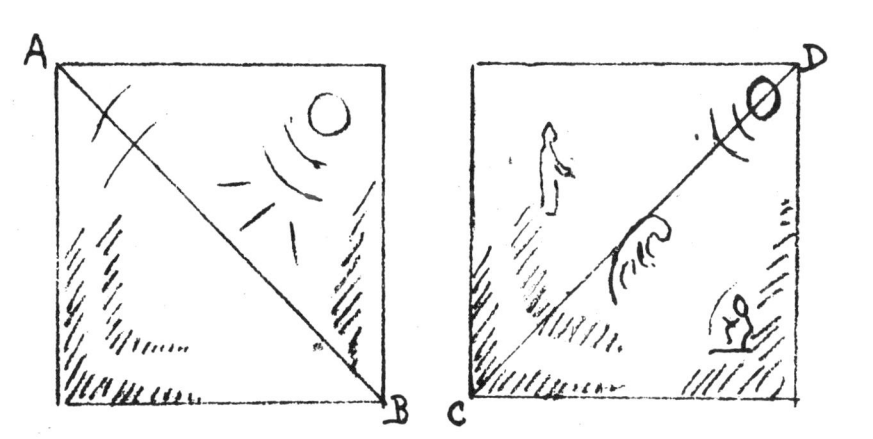

So that to the right of and under the diagonal c–d, we see everything which, in substance and treatment, belongs to the earth, to the left of and above it, everything which in the same sense belongs to Heaven. The Druid priest, standing erect, turns towards the radiance, absorbed in contemplation of the higher gods, freed from the purely earthly. Over him in the clouds (which might well be the Hosts of the Hierarchies) soars the Cross in yellow, distinct and recognizable, as it were a delicate allusion to the Christ event, which at that time was slowly approaching. Behind the upper Druid and bursting forth from the dark earth on which he stands, a rainbow raises its arc to the sun, joining and reconciling Heaven and Earth.

So, through these diagonals we see—twice—the heavenly divided from the earthly; through diagonal *a–b* in a colourful, light-and-shade sense, through *c–d* in the sense of content and treatment. Laid over one another, *a–b* and *c–d* form a St Andrew's cross, towards which this whole picture is secretly pointing. Exactly at the intersection of the two diagonals, a second Druid priest stands before his altar, not upright but bending downwards. What the upper priest has absorbed and drawn down into himself of the radiance of the sunlit, cosmic powers is transmitted by the second priest for its right use to the simple, uninitiated men of the community in the valley, entrusted to his care, and this is indicated by the direction of his glance, the position of his arms and the posture of his body bending to the earth. These powers of the sun and the heavens, which every man bears within him in his four-petalled lotus flowers, significantly appear also at the altar of the lower Druid. So this second Druid actually stands in the sense indicated by both diagonals at the point of intersection where the heavenly and divine come into contact with the earthly and human.

Over each Druid hovers his aura, that of the initiate, in gentle movement, which later, with the Romanizing of the spiritual, was represented as the dead, rigid, circular halo.

It must also be added that the men of the time depicted here built no temples containing images of the gods chiselled from stone. Instead they sought rock formations in nature, which reminded them of the forms of those gods whom they venerated. And so too in this picture: beginning at the last of the three upper altar stones on the right, there is plainly recognizable the profile of a dignified old man, sitting with his hands clasped round his knees and looking straight before him deep in thought. Just on his knees is the single altar with the four-petalled lotus flower. This place actually exists on the English coast. It is further known that these old mystery-centres found in modern England were dedicated to Jupiter and served the Jupiter wisdom. The old priests sought for the building of their centres of worship those parts of the land which were already specially suited for their purpose, where the rock formations contained the ore of the metal associated with the forces of the planet whose deity they wished to honour. Now Jupiter is associated with tin, and so it is understandable that these centres of worship were always erected on rocks rich in tin.

'In this picture, this tin-bearing rock whose stone induces devotion, because of its substance, is depicted in blue, which further down passes into a dull red, the red indicating the warmth of the volcanic forces rising from below. At the left and right edges is shown the dead black of the barren stone devoid of tin, which in this sense has no relationship to the Godhead and on which the tin-bearing rocks rest.'

The Picture by the Painter Claudius Jaquand

In a lecture on 'Rosicrucian Christianity' given in Neuchâtel on 27 September 1911, Rudolf Steiner speaks about the upbringing of Christian Rosenkreutz by the twelve initiates in the thirteenth century. In the course of this lecture Dr Steiner describes how the spiritual forces of Christian Rosenkreutz grew ever greater and his physical forces dwindled away until he finally died of starvation. Now there is a very interesting painting which some friends saw in the museum of a Central European town some decades ago. On a subsequent visit in the fifties the picture had disappeared. An elderly museum curator said to them that it was no longer allowed to be shown to the public, but he took them into the cellar where the picture was stored and they were even allowed to have a reproduction of it. The friends have since died and have bequeathed this picture to me. Everyone to whom I showed it was very impressed and begged me to let them have a photograph of it. When one knows the lecture mentioned above, a connection springs to mind between what is here portrayed as *The death by starvation of Count Gaston de Foix* and the description of Christian Rosenkreutz given by Rudolf Steiner. The painter of this picture is called Claudius Jaquand and he lived 1804–78.

I might allude here to the triptych by Anna May called *The Grail* which has the same theme.

*The death by starvation of Count Gaston de Foix
by Claudius Jaquand*

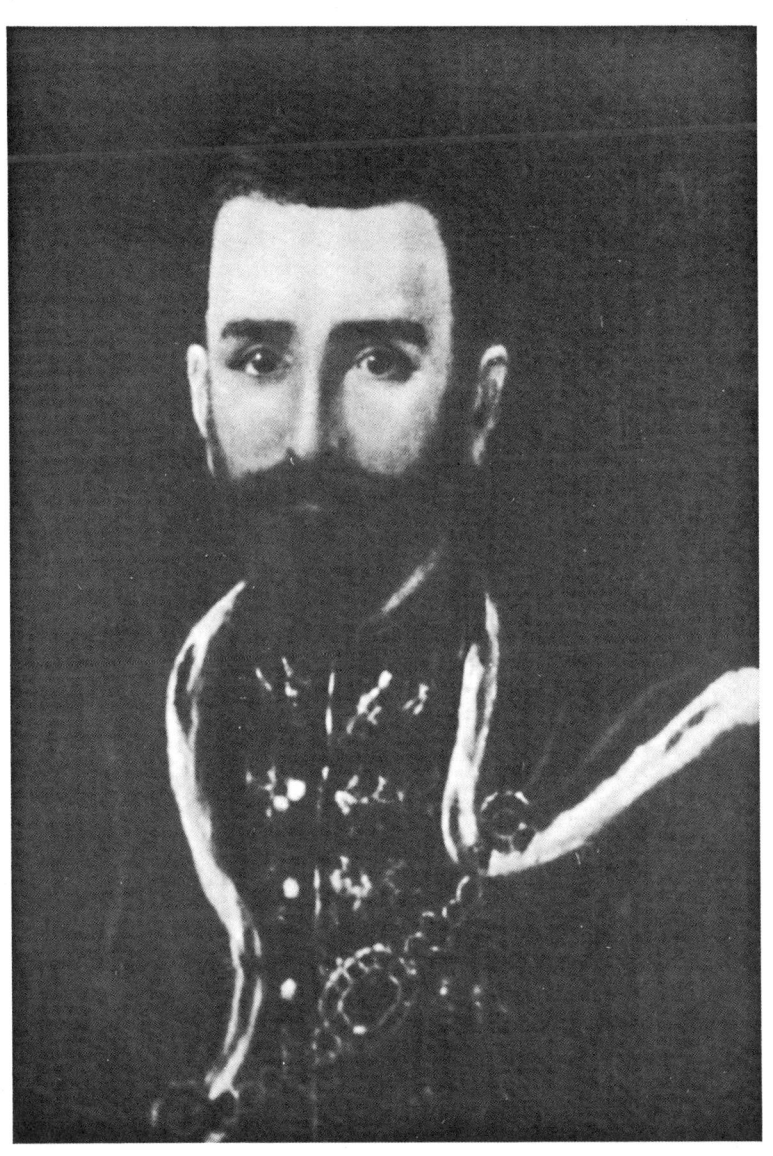

Christian Rosenkreutz

The Picture of Christian Rosenkreutz

This picture was given to Helene Röchling by Rudolf Steiner, who told her that it portrays Christian Rosenkreutz. As far as I can discover it is unknown. Those to whom I showed it were deeply impressed by it. I present it here so that as many people as possible may get to know it.

16. Episodes

First come two episodes which I should not like to forego. The one took place in Mannheim before a lecture which Dr Steiner was about to give. I stood next to him as he was entering the hall. There in front of him stood an elderly gentleman whom the doorkeeper did not wish to admit until he had first handed in his coat to the attendant. Very sadly the man said that in that case he would have to go away again. Dr Steiner then asked him why he did not want to give up his coat and the man replied that he had no jacket underneath. It was just after the war and things of that sort were commonplace. There was really nothing to be ashamed of about it. Dr Steiner said to the doorkeeper that he was the lecturer and that it was his wish that the man should be admitted. The doorkeeper, who would willingly have complied, said however that such a thing was strictly against the rules and he stood to lose his job if he disobeyed them. Then Dr Steiner promised on his part that he would vouch for him if necessary but that the man had to be admitted otherwise he would not give his lecture.

When he was at home again Dr Steiner explained that it was of great importance for just this man to be present when he spoke. He always scrutinized his audience very carefully and often directed what he had to say to the one or other person. Thus he said to us one day after a lecture in Dornach: 'You must have wondered why I seemingly deviated so much today from the theme we had in hand. There was someone in the hall who made it necessary for me to avoid certain topics. He would have misinterpreted what I said and that would have caused difficulties. I shall return to the theme I had in mind another time.'

There is another episode which is characteristic of the way Dr Steiner reacted under certain circumstances. During the after-war years we eurythmists used to eat together with Herr and Frau Dr Steiner in the Motzstrasse in Berlin where we were catered for by Frau Walther who prepared our meals from the little that was to be had at that time in a loving and careful manner. On one such occasion Dr Steiner turned to the eurythmist sitting beside him and asked her to say the grace. With embarrassment she had to confess that she did not know it off by heart and so it was the turn of the next one and the one after her and so on. And when finally most of those present had been unable to fulfil this task Dr Steiner said to me, who he knew could do it: 'Well, Ilona, will you say the verse for us?' This grace is the one given by Dr Steiner: 'The plant seeds are quickened...' The eurythmists would have been able to say other verses off by heart but Dr Steiner said it was important always to use this verse as he had given it for that purpose. After the meal everyone busily set about learning this verse. Next day Dr Steiner said straight away, 'Please say grace for us Ilona.' All the others now said that they had learned it but Dr Steiner said: 'Now it is too late. For the rest of our stay here Ilona will be the one to say it.'

Another thing that Dr Steiner was very strict about was that no high spiritual matters should be discussed at table, such as for instance the content of lectures or even esoteric topics.

As I have just been speaking about saying grace I can add another little story in the same vein. When I was a small child I had a little prayer hanging over my bed surrounded by Angels. I used to say this prayer every night and when I could not get to sleep straight away I used to try to say it off by heart backwards. That stuck with me so that I can still repeat it to this day. On one particular occasion Dr Steiner happened to mention that small children often write and speak backwards and I chirped up and said that I too used to do that and I immediately said my back-to-front prayer for him. Dr Steiner found that so nice that I had to say it three times one after another. Then he said, 'Ah yes, you have still carried something with you from the spiritual world.' I then told him that at a later date when I was feeling bored with my lessons, as happened occasionally, I tried to learn pieces of music back-to-front. He thought that was a very good exercise, though perhaps not practised on quite the right occasion!

The dress rehearsal for a performance in a cinema theatre in Hilversum had been arranged to take place in the morning. We had arrived somewhat early and the film technicians were still busy trying something out for the afternoon programme so we were asked to wait for a while in the auditorium. We watched their film about the manufacture of porcelain and it was not long before they rolled up the screen and we could start our rehearsal. When the first item began we all experienced a strange kind of paralysis; we could hardly move our limbs and felt as if a part of us was dead. Dr Steiner then came into the room and we made our complaints to him. He said to us: 'Why of course! Now you will have to get rid of the ahrimanic-mechanical effects of the "cinema-affair". All of you get up onto the stage and do the standing "Hallelujah", that is a way to "clean" the atmosphere in any room and drive away any bad influences.' We immediately put it into practice and it really had a remarkable effect. We felt a noticeable relief.

The 'Hallelujah' which Dr Steiner expressed—'Cleanse me of all influences which hinder me from seeing the Godhead'—can be used by the individual if the sounds are formed with the necessary reverence and in peacefulness of mind. Then one arrives at inner harmony and aspiration for the spirit. One can be aware of how the urge to cling to what is too earthly and egoistic then falls away from one. I have made use of it later on similar occasions and it always helped. Dr Steiner gave instructions for the 'Hallelujah' to be performed in various ways in eurythmy performances.

To the foregoing episodes I should like to add one or two remarks. We were at lunch in the Landhausstrasse in Stuttgart. The dessert was fruit. Dr Steiner took an apple and suddenly stopped as he was peeling it to enquire: 'Who can divide an apple in half three-dimensionally?' Now began a great deal of experimenting—more and more apples were demanded till a great pile of them had collected on the table. Frau Doktor commented that we would have enough stewed apple to last us a week. Finally Dr Steiner took pity on us and showed us how to do it. Herr Dr Unger, whom we told about it next day, laughed and said, 'That is not very difficult to do,' and he divided the apple correctly without any hesitation. Those who had been at table the previous day had all been unable to do it. Some of them had certainly been secretly practising at home!

During breaks between rehearsals or when we were travelling, Dr Steiner often used to compare human beings with animals. Thus on one occasion we were standing behind the stage in the Workshop talking together happily when Dr Steiner passed by. He listened to us for a while, then, putting on his pince-nez, he looked down the line and turning to Annemarie Dubach he said, 'Yes, you are a swallow.' Then to Frau de Jaager he said, 'You, however, are a phoenix. And turning to me he said laughingly, 'And you, well you are a sparrow!' Probably I looked a little disappointed at that, so he said in a kindly way, 'But a very dear one!'

On another occasion he compared Fräulein Waller to a floating dandelion seed and Frau Röchling to a head of chicory. My mother was compared to a snapdragon blossom, Fräulein Mucke to a mallow blossom and I to a pinkish yellow rosebud. These characterizations were so apt that all those present were astonished and said: 'Yes, we've all got something of that about us but we would not have hit upon it ourselves.'

17. Eurythmy Lessons with Children from 3 to 7 Years

Dr Steiner gave some directions for eurythmy lessons with children between the ages of 3 and 7 which I would here like to include because I am always being asked about it. Thus he said that it would be good to do eurythmy as far as possible to music. First one should activate the legs more, then more the arms, then both together. One should explore the various ways of putting the feet on the ground, how strongly or how gently one treads when one uses one's legs. Only after that has been exercised should the children step to rhythm, then mark the beat with the arms and afterwards do both together. For instance: 'Big clocks go tack-tack-tack' = long steps; 'Little clocks go ticka-ticka-ticka' = short steps. Repeat this many times in succession and then do the equivalent with the arms and hands. The sounds are done with the children, first the vowels, then the

Eurythmy with children

consonants. It is better in this case too to do it to music. Later on the sounds can be incorporated into little stories.

It will be best here to give a short account of how I managed such a lesson. I first let the children do various kinds of stepping—firm, stamping steps while going round in a circle, then quiet, even steps still quite slowly, then gradually quickening until the children break into a run, and then changing again into a slow pace. Following that the children should walk on tiptoe so quietly that it cannot be heard. I sometimes also let the children walk forwards and backwards in a line holding hands and making sure that none of them pushes forward in front of another. If that should occur (as it is bound to do, of course) then the 'pushers' can be put into an extra row to do the exercises alone, then certain of them are picked out to rejoin the slower ones, and finally all can try it together once more. This exercise always gave us great pleasure. One lesson may be taken up with doing the exercises just described, another devoted more to rhythmic exercises. With the latter, one should also start first with the feet—a lot of long steps to begin with, then only short steps until one is *almost* marking time, then one *only* marks time. After that the rhythm should change to a short and a long step, whereby the teacher makes clear (by example) that it is the *timing* which must be precise. Rhythmic exercises should also be done to music. The accompanist must employ a lot of imagination and the class must react to it quickly when the music is played either loudly or softly, firmly or delicately, quickly or slowly.

The 'I' 'A' 'O' (ee—ah—oh) exercise

Where is your head?—'Hier' (head erect)
Where are your legs?—'Da' (jump with legs apart)
What are your arms doing?—'So' (make an 'O' with the arms)

Then lower arms, jump with legs together, lower head.

Or, in a slightly adapted English version:

Where is your head?—Here
What do your legs say?—Ah!
What is in your arms?—Gold

I did that exercise at the beginning of every lesson. I also did the three parts simultaneously.

We first learned the sounds standing in a circle, then practised them through children's songs or poems. The charming poems by Hedwig Diester and Marianne Garf, for instance, are especially suitable. Later on I progressed to little stories that I made up myself. For instance: 'Today we are going for a walk. Who is coming with us?' Then from all sides one could hear: 'Ich, ich, ich' [ee—ee—ee]—a splendid 'ee' sound! Then we lift a sack onto our backs with 'B' or 'P' and stump off with 'short-long' or 'long-short' steps or in some other rhythm. We come to a meadow where there are a lot of flowers [Blumen or Blümchen] 'BL', or 'U', or 'Ü'. We smell them [riechen] CH and the scent [Duft] gives us 'D'. Every child has a different flower which is expressed in eurythmy. Of course the little hare is not lacking, which happily hops about (according to a well-known poem). And, oh shame on me if by the end of the lesson I should happen to step on a place where a flower had stood. Then one of the children might cry out: 'Oh Miss, you are trampling on the flower,' or on the little hare, or whatever we had conjured up so beautifully.

Sometimes we climbed a mountain before sunrise with many different kinds of step or rhythm. Arrived at the summit we stood in a mood of devotion—the gesture for 'devotion' changing to an expectant admiring 'A' [ah] until the sun came up. But then we were so dazzled that we had to hide behind an 'E' [eh]. After that we could say a prayer or say or sing a little poem or song referring to the sun.

On still another occasion we were dwarfs bent forward with heavy, clumsy steps as we entered into the mountain where we hammered at the veins of silver and gold and broke off beautiful crystals which we stuffed into our little satchels we had with us—all done to appropriate sounds—then happily going homeward. We danced in the meadows with the elves, were whirled around in the air by the wind, splashed in the water and were washed by the waves. All this took place whenever possible to music.

The songs from Humperdink's *Hansel and Gretel* were very popular, for instance: '*Brüderlein komm tanz mit mir*' [Little brother come and dance with me], '*Abend wenn ich schlafen geh*' [In the evening when I go to sleep], and 'The Song of the Sandman'.

This, of course, is teaching material for many lessons and one has to choose and arrange one's lesson according to the situation at the time. Half an hour goes by very quickly and one should not do eurythmy with small children for more than that length of time according to Dr Steiner. If one reckons with a whole hour that would include changing of shoes, etc. and the greeting which plays a significant part in the proceedings.

It occasionally happened that a child would flatly refuse to join in. In this instance I would take it by the hand and do the rhythm with it in that way. I can still remember a very delicate and shy little girl who stood by the wall the whole lesson long with her arms behind her back and a grim look on her face and could not be persuaded to move from there. Her mother told me that at home when she thought she was unobserved she would imitate everything and could do it very nicely. The mother brought the child to the lesson valiantly and faithfully again and again until one fine day she joined in quite naturally and as a matter of course. She later became an excellent eurythmist!

It should be stressed that no intellectual explanations should be given to children before the seventh year. Everything should remain in the realm of play so that they have pleasure in the pictures that one paints for them in eurythmy. But the teacher herself must demonstrate her eurythmy outwardly as clearly and distinctly as she experiences it inwardly, then by imitation the children will acquire it for themselves.

In whatever I did with the children I have always been very careful to make every movement as exact and distinct as possible. The children appreciate that more than one imagines. On a later occasion when I had to deputize in a class of 12–14 year old boys and wanted to do some rhythms with them some of them complained that doing rhythms was *so* boring and demonstrated it accordingly—it really was terrible! Then I showed them how Dr Steiner visualized rhythm, and gave them eurythmy rods to use as swords and told them to ride forth as knights into battle. They did that excellently to a short-long or short-short-long rhythm and had great fun with it. The stricter I was about being exact, the more they liked it. They themselves discovered new possibilities and became more imaginative in the process.

18. Remarks by Dr Steiner about the Twelve Virtues

With regard to the twelve virtues and their connection with the zodiac and the months, Dr Steiner said in a private conversation that H.P. Blavatsky was the one who pointed to the affinity between the virtues and the months in the order and designation as below:

Ram	= April	= Devotion
Bull	= May	= Equilibrium
Twins	= June	= Endurance
Crab	= July	= Selflessness
Lion	= August	= Compassion
Virgin	= September	= Politeness
Scales	= October	= Contentment
Scorpion	= November	= Patience
Archer	= December	= Control of Thinking
Goat	= January	= Courage
Water Carrier	= February	= Discretion
Fishes	= March	= Magnanimity

Dr Steiner confirmed this sequence but then added the following information. He said: 'If one practises these virtues conscientiously, new forces and abilities will grow out of them.' Then he listed these in the following way:

Devotion	Force of Sacrifice
Equilibrium	Progress
Endurance	Faithfulness
Selflessness	Catharsis
Compassion	Independence
Politeness	Tactfulness of Heart
Contentment	Calmness
Patience	Insight
Control of Thinking	Feeling for Truth
Courage	Power of Redemption
Discretion	Meditative Power
Magnanimity	Love

To conclude, Dr Steiner said: 'Always begin to practise a virtue on the 21st of the month preceding it and continue till the 1st of the month after it, i.e. Devotion from 21 March–May, etc. The fact that the time allotted to each exercise overlaps the dates given for the zodiac need not be considered in this case. One should just practise the virtue of Devotion during April always beginning, as stated, on the 21st of the preceding month.'

As the result of my endeavour over the years to follow these instructions, a picture has presented itself to me of a retrograde loop encompassing the past and bringing it into the present while at the same time the future is also incorporated, so that past, present and future work into one another.

19. Meditation for the Sick and Dying

Together with the Heinrich-Lanz Hospital in Mannheim, the Lanz Military Hospital was endowed and established through the initiative of Helene Röchling during the war years 1914–18. She had asked many of the older and younger women members of the Society to work in it with her. The running of the house, laundry, kitchen, etc. was placed under their management and they tackled what were often difficult tasks with devotion. Helene Röchling was loved by all of them in spite of her great strictness, and not only by them but also especially by the soldiers whom she frequently visited and for whom she occasionally wrote letters, encouraged them and lovingly shared in their worries and needs. There was hardly one of them who turned to her in vain. It gave her pain to think that she could do so little to help the severely ill or dying. So she turned to Dr Steiner for advice. He recommended specific meditations to her for the night-watch when she was allowed to take over duty for the sisters. This is how the following verse came to be written:

(*Directed towards the other person*)
    Flow blood,
    Work through the flowing,

>   Stirring muscle,
>   Stir the Life-germ.
>   Loving care
>   Of warming hearts
>   Be healing Breath.

> (*For oneself, as if talking to oneself*)
>   So long as thou dost feel the pain
>   Which I am spared,
>   The Christ unrecognized
>   Is working in the world.
>   For weak is still the Spirit
>   While each is only capable of suffering
>   Through his own body.*

How much suffering Frau Röchling helped to assuage—sometimes easing the crossing of the Threshold for the dying!

To express her recognition of the faithful service given by her colleagues she ordered a pendant to be made and asked Dr Steiner for a design for it. He made a drawing and wrote the words: *Heil den Helfern der Heilung* [Hail to the Helpers of Healing]. The illustration here reproduced [p. 88] shows the medallion which is still in my possession.

20. Remarks by Dr Steiner Concerning Pregnancy and the Care of Young Children

While I was pregnant I had to give up doing eurythmy because a child needs the etheric forces of its mother. I was allowed to give lessons provided I did not do the movements myself. After the child is born the mother should abstain from doing eurythmy for one

---

* These two meditations are to be found in GA 157 in the German, and 'Thoughts for the Times' in English, lecture on 1 September 1914 given in Berlin. The instructions in brackets above the meditations were noted by Frau Röchling.

year—not, as is often maintained, for *three* years. Dr Steiner based this statement on the fact that until the child has completed its first year it is still very much connected to the etheric body of the mother and needs those forces. But I was allowed to see a lot of eurythmy performances and listen to good music wherever possible and look at beautiful pictures. I also assiduously attended lectures and read a great number of them. Meditation was allowed within certain bounds. For instance, I was present at the Christmas Gathering in 1923 and have never missed any of the special events. I emphasize that particularly because at a later time I heard that Dr Steiner had once forbidden another lady to read difficult lectures or to meditate, or at any rate advised her not to do so.

Certain scenes from *Faust* are also to be avoided during pregnancy, such as for instance 'The Prologue in Heaven' because of the discussion between the Lord and Mephistopheles. Also, the scene with the Lamiae and those with the Phorkyads have a very harmful effect. And the scenes in the Christmas plays are to be avoided where the Devil appears and where Herod is shown. In connection to that is the directive that one should avoid funerals or cremation services and that it is not good to go for walks with small children through cemeteries. It is of course quite evident that one does not go to the cinema during this time, or read—or even look at—illustrated newspapers, which would be particularly harmful. All this should be perfectly understandable. A health-giving and beneficial result is obtained by gazing at the picture of a Madonna before going to sleep, the most suitable one being the *Sistine Madonna*, and it is good on first waking to let the eye rest on this picture.

If one listens very carefully on waking one can make out the name of the child from the fifth month onward. I asked Dr Steiner if he would give me a name for my child. When my little boy was born I had to wait another three days until Dr Steiner sent me a note to the clinic with the name on it. The authorities had already complained that the name had to be produced and if absolutely no name was forthcoming then I should settle for Hans, Fritz or Otto, which were all quite nice names. When Dr Steiner was informed of this he said: 'Yes, I will give you the name as soon as his Angel tells it to me, one has to be patient in such a case.' But on the third day he sent me two names and the authorities were satisfied.

When I asked Dr Steiner what I should eat during pregnancy, he

Medallion, 'Hail to the Helpers of Healing'
(the illustration is reproduced double the size of the original)

said: 'Eat anything you fancy. It is good to eat a lot of vegetables, especially cauliflower, because it stimulates the flow of milk. It is better to avoid sharp things and not to touch walnuts or hazelnuts.' Of course smoking is very injurious.

Bending down and stretching upwards too much, as in hanging out clothes, should be avoided. Women who are accustomed to hard physical work should take especial care. When winding wool or mixing batter one should not concentrate too hard on what one is doing but think about something more pleasant. 'That was known to our grandmothers who instinctively felt and did things in a much healthier way.' To go for walks in the fresh air is very good but they should not last too long at a time, especially during the later stages (a quarter of an hour at this time corresponds to about an hour under normal conditions). It is good to avoid sitting with crossed legs or folded arms. The same applies when one is meditating or listening to a mantram as has already been mentioned [pp. 20–21].

Do not travel more than is absolutely necessary. Restrict the amount of car journeying too.

And here I should add that it is a good thing to rub the nipples every day with alcohol, for instance, or lemon juice or eau de Cologne. That will strengthen them.

When the child is born it should lie in the same room as the mother, if possible. Mother and child are usually put into separate rooms in hospitals, which is not good. It is just while the child is so very young that it and the mother should be together as much as possible. The baby also needs to be kept much warmer than people usually imagine. When Dr Steiner once visited me after I was back from hospital he said to me on entering the room: 'But the baby is much too cold.' I was very surprised because I had only just asked for the window to be opened as I was feeling too hot, but because of the visit it had been left as it was. Dr Steiner said to me: 'Give me double the amount of clothing he has on at present.' Then he took off all its wrappings and bound it up again in double the amount of things. I might however add that one should not overdo it as I once saw happen! Children should not lie bathed in sweat. And now, after Dr Steiner had wrapped the child up again, he took it in his arms, walked up and down with it and said, 'See how well it feels now.' When I had to visit the clinic the following week for an operation the child had to go with me. As I was unable to feed it myself it had a bottle which

I gave it myself so that I could be with it as much as possible.

When I was back at home again Dr Steiner advised me to put the child in its pram in the garden or on the terrace when it was warm enough, but told me not to wheel it about in the pram but to carry it in its 'pillow-bag' as one used to do in the olden days, then it would experience the same rhythm as when it was in the womb. When the child is in the open air it should always wear a little bonnet; this could be a light lace cap. It is good if the fontanelle only closes slowly; the possibilities for spiritual development will then be all the greater. For this same reason it is necessary to hang a thin gauze veil over the cot or pram. Dr Steiner usually prescribed the colour for this veil. If the mother herself does not know which colour to choose, a light blue is always suitable.

Children should have their sleep at regular times. Do not lift them too often during the night, but on the other hand do not let them lie in wet nappies too long. One should not let the child be on its own too long during the day either. When the child is awake one can sing to it a little, take it in one's arms and carry it about for a while.

One should never quarrel in the child's presence or carry on animated conversations, as is also the case with older children. Sunbathing and infant gymnastics should be avoided completely just as one should also avoid 'hardening' children, as this leads to early sclerosis and materialism. It is all right to let the child cry now and again as that develops moral forces. Of course one cannot always allow that to happen and the mother herself should know when it is permissible and under what circumstances.

Most of these instructions apply to the first child. As soon as there are brothers and sisters much of this rights itself.

Sucking dummies is very bad for children as it makes them sensual in later life. If a child wants to suck something it should suck its own thumb, but the earlier it can be weaned from this habit the better. The child should not have more than two or three baths a week. On other days it should have a good wash only. If the water is very hard one should put a little bag of bran in the bath. Too many baths make a child nervous, and to let a baby do too much kicking produces a similar effect.

Dr Steiner advised that *all* people, both young and old, should avoid sunbathing as this destroys the etheric forces. The wearing of socks is not good either and a child would be better off running about with bare feet. Of course one would often have to put up with remonstrances from the child, but if one could succeed in achieving this it would certainly be an advantage.

If children are afraid of being alone at night it is best to put a night-light in the room and one should say a prayer even with the youngest of children at bedtime, for even if they do not understand the words it will be absorbed into the soul. Likewise a prayer should be said before meals. In later years the children must learn to say the prayer themselves, but they should not be forced into it, rather they should learn it quite naturally by hearing it spoken every day. 'Whoever does not learn to pray as a child will not be able to bless in old age,' added Dr Steiner.

What follows has to do with infant diet. When my child was small there were not so many ready-made baby foods about as there are today. So we had to develop ideas of our own and be able to sense what was good for the child and what it enjoyed. I gave mine little snacks made with rusks or *Paidol* [trade name?] and later groats or semolina pudding (not always sweetened) and when sweetened Dr Steiner advised me to use *Nutromalt*. From half a year onwards I gave him carrots, spinach or plenty of mashed vegetables and a lot of fruit juice. He was given no eggs at all before his third year and only very few after that until he was seven. The child should preferably eat all that is on its plate but must not be forced to do so, otherwise it would lose its natural instinct.

Choleric children become calmer if they are given a lot of red to wear or are put into red surroundings. For phlegmatic children on the other hand blue is the best remedy. Inner growing forces are stimulated by outer impressions or can be inhibited as the case may be. The more one can provide good examples for the child to copy the better it will be. 'The habits of the mother become capacities in the child.' Children should not watch eurythmy performances too early in life and above all the programme should not be too long.

All these suggestions should not be adhered to too rigidly, only in so far as outward circumstances permit! The most important thing is to surround the child with love all the time.

* * *

I would next like to relate what happened at the Christening of my son Christward Johannes because that too shows so much of Dr

Steiner's character. It was in our room that the ceremony was enacted in the house of Frau Wirz which is the present 'Schiefer' boarding-house. We had decorated the room very beautifully with flowers and the altar stood beneath the 'Milan' Christ picture. My son wore a traditional light blue Christening gown and was in a 'carrying-cushion' of the same colour. It had been worn in our family for generations and looked very festive and splendid. To my dismay the child cried a lot during the service and afterwards Dr Steiner said to me: 'Yes, he was hungry.' I told him that he had had his bottle just before the Christening but Dr Steiner said, 'Nevertheless he was hungry. Get him another bottle straight away.' I was a little afraid that it might not be good for him because the ward sister had told me not to give him too much to drink. But when the bottle was ready Dr Steiner took the child on his lap, sat down comfortably in the armchair and fed it himself, and the bottle was empty in no time. 'You see, he is happy now and is laughing. Give him an extra bottle from me every day.' It did the child a lot of good and he throve splendidly.

A few days later a phone message came from Dr Steiner to ask me to come to him with the child. I had hardly got there when he took it in his arms and went into his room. It was long before those two reappeared, Dr Steiner with Christward Johannes, and he asked for the child to be brought to him again and again.

How fond Dr Steiner was of children altogether. How nice when he joked with them or when he talked to them quite seriously. He often asked them riddles and was very pleased when they were able to answer them. Often he would also ask the grown-ups riddles, some of which he made up himself and others which he took from the famous 'Brentano' collection. While we were travelling on our never-ending eurythmy tours it helped to pass the time for us. One of the riddles which Dr Steiner set for Fräulein Scholl was the following:

In the *first* search for the universal ground and goal of existence.
You strive towards the *second* in order to realize yourself as Man.
Think about the *whole* and you will realize
how Man raises himself up to the *first*.